MW00447832

Justice Seekers

Justice Seekers

Pursuing Equity in the Details of Teaching and Learning

Lacey Robinson

JB JOSSEY-BASS™
A Wiley Brand

Copyright © 2023 by UnboundEd Learning. All rights reserved.

Published by John Wiley & Sons, Inc., Hoboken, New Jersey.
Published simultaneously in Canada.

No part of this publication may be reproduced, stored in a retrieval system, or transmitted in any form or by any means, electronic, mechanical, photocopying, recording, scanning, or otherwise, except as permitted under Section 107 or 108 of the 1976 United States Copyright Act, without either the prior written permission of the Publisher, or authorization through payment of the appropriate per-copy fee to the Copyright Clearance Center, Inc., 222 Rosewood Drive, Danvers, MA 01923, (978) 750-8400, fax (978) 750-4470, or on the web at www.copyright.com. Requests to the Publisher for permission should be addressed to the Permissions Department, John Wiley & Sons, Inc., 111 River Street, Hoboken, NJ 07030, (201) 748-6011, fax (201) 748-6008, or online at www.wiley.com/go/permission.

Trademarks: Wiley and the Wiley logo are trademarks or registered trademarks of John Wiley & Sons, Inc. and/or its affiliates in the United States and other countries and may not be used without written permission. All other trademarks are the property of their respective owners. John Wiley & Sons, Inc. is not associated with any product or vendor mentioned in this book.

Limit of Liability/Disclaimer of Warranty: While the publisher and author have used their best efforts in preparing this book, they make no representations or warranties with respect to the accuracy or completeness of the contents of this book and specifically disclaim any implied warranties of merchantability or fitness for a particular purpose. No warranty may be created or extended by sales representatives or written sales materials. The advice and strategies contained herein may not be suitable for your situation. You should consult with a professional where appropriate. Neither the publisher nor author shall be liable for any loss of profit or any other commercial damages, including but not limited to special, incidental, consequential, or other damages. Further, readers should be aware that websites listed in this work may have changed or disappeared between when this work was written and when it is read.

For general information on our other products and services or for technical support, please contact our Customer Care Department within the United States at (800) 762-2974, outside the United States at (317) 572-3993 or fax (317) 572-4002.

Wiley also publishes its books in a variety of electronic formats. Some content that appears in print may not be available in electronic formats. For more information about Wiley products, visit our web site at www.wiley.com.

Library of Congress Cataloging-in-Publication Data:

Names: Robinson, Lacey, author.
Title: Justice seekers : pursuing equity in the details of teaching and
   learning / Lacey Robinson.
Description: Hoboken, New Jersey : Jossey-Bass, [2023] | Includes index.
Identifiers: LCCN 2023003268 (print) | LCCN 2023003269 (ebook) | ISBN
   9781394189724 (paperback) | ISBN 9781394189748 (adobe pdf) | ISBN
   9781394189755 (epub)
Subjects: LCSH: Educational equalization. | Education—Social aspects.
Classification: LCC LC213 .R64 2023 (print) | LCC LC213 (ebook) | DDC
   379.2/6—dc23/eng/20230221
LC record available at https://lccn.loc.gov/2023003268
LC ebook record available at https://lccn.loc.gov/2023003269

Cover Art: © Getty Images | Jeff Seltzer Photography
Cover Design: Paul McCarthy

SKY10048203_051823

CONTENTS

CONTENTS

INTRODUCTION

It was 301 days after the announcement of the pandemic—an event that seemed to unleash a cyclone of social, political, racial, and humanitarian crises across the world—and I was sitting at the kitchen counter working on my laptop, the TV news rolling in the background. On the morning of January 6, 2021, like me, many educators were logging onto their laptops. Others, in districts or states where policies mandated that they must enter their school buildings and offices despite the uncertain safety conditions they were braving as new COVID-19 variants emerged, teachers were wiping down desks and spraying disinfectant. Many were oblivious to what was unfolding, not just in our country's capital, but in state capitals around the nation.

I sat at my makeshift counter workspace that day astounded by the insurrection. I wished I was seeing some epic scene in a historical action movie, but it was real life, a democracy unraveling before our eyes on social media posts, TVs, and radio announcements. Honestly, those January 6th scenes felt like a breaking open, a dramatic and sudden exposure of so many of the ills that our country had been hiding for decades, even centuries before. Months and years of civic and racial unrest lingered in the air. The sound of George Floyd calling for his mother as well as the marches for Trayvon Martin, Sandra Bland, Freddie Gray, Breonna Taylor, and countless others were top of mind. Like many of us, I watched as the insurrectionists broke past police lines and pushed democracy to the edge of an abyss. As an educator, my mind went right to our students and what they were witnessing. What messages were being affirmed or discounted about our nation as they watched armed men, women, young and old attempt to overthrow a national election? Who was being triggered by the violence and rage? What level of safety did our students feel witnessing civil unrest at such a large scale?

I began to think about a conversation I had overheard at the grocery store weeks before. A young man and his mother were checking out ahead of me. He was examining a magazine with a headline highlighting the dangers of global warming and enticing the reader to look within to find out what they could do to help.

As he put the magazine back he quipped to his mother, "We won't even be around in the next 50 years. Why does this matter?" I remembered feeling the sting of hopelessness and an educator's urge to jump into the conversation and encourage him to analyze what he had just said. As I stood in that checkout line, the feeling of his despair blanketed me.

As I watched the insurrection unfold on January 6th, I wondered what he—and all the students like him showing up to their Zoom and in-person classrooms—felt as they witnessed this moment in history. If January 6, 2021, shined an undeniable spotlight on the cracks and fissures in our entire society, I wondered what role education could play in mending those gaps.

While the most acute pressure from the education system's structural instability can be felt at the classroom level, we needed a framework to help educators address just how deeply and widely these injustices had spread. When I first became a public school teacher in 1996, I learned pretty early on that those in positions of power, both within and outside the school system, were making decisions that, at best, affected their quarterly assessments and, at worst, affected the minute-to-minute, day-to-day actions and planning of educators in school buildings. Even when I held positions at the district level later in my career, my skills were leveraged into what was deemed pertinent for the newest endeavor, not into addressing the systemic inequities I'd witnessed for years and at every level.

It was at the system level—sitting in meetings where leaders were making decisions regarding materials, products, programs, and hiring practices that would play a role in either supporting our students' careers and college trajectories or hindering them—where I finally began to see the machine behind the cloak of the public school system. I quickly understood that the decisions being made were not always grounded in the research and evaluation cycle. Instead, decisions were birthed from political views, relationships, and, of course, funding. I was disappointed to realize how little system leaders utilized the research and development that were necessary to eradicate harmful conditions for students who experienced the greatest disenfranchisement through food, housing, and economic insecurities.

Justice is found in the details of teaching and learning® was born out of those experiences and the experiences of the many educators at UnboundEd who wanted to take a different approach to transforming education for Black, brown, and Indigenous children. Years ago at UnboundEd—an national nonprofit I've led since 2019, after 23 years as an educator—we began a journey to address how those fissures showed up in the work of education. In frank conversations, we released our own shame about complicity in upholding the system as it is, and we read the research about how to combat the systemic inequities that had both benefited and harmed us. Through this process we began to see a path forward. At the center of that path is an understanding that moments like January 6, 2021, happen when we refuse to fully wrestle with our sordid past as a nation as it relates to racism and to our failed systems. Most importantly, we have not as a nation faced the ways these failures influence our thinking and understanding of the world around us.

We live in a time in our society in which information cycles at a pace few people could have anticipated decades ago. Partly because it's so hard to sift through all of that information, I believe we have retrained ourselves to trust the word that is shuffled among us, online and in conversation, rather than the word that lives on paper, as a result of review and verification. Even as more information streams into our lives, most people will leave high school having learned to read only moderately. Moderate readers may at times find themselves relying more on the word that was passed to them rather than on what they could read. So, at a time when critical analysis and thought are more crucial than ever, we have a crisis of functional illiteracy in our country. According to a 2020 Gallup analysis, 54% of adults lack proficiency in literacy.[1] Few times in my adult life have I felt that crisis more acutely than in the moments leading up to and away from that January 6th morning. And as much as the harrowing moments that have shaped our past few years have been about political and societal systems, they have also been American education's failure to produce a truly literate society, one that embraces robust critical thought and creates equitable outcomes for every one of its citizens.

Of course, education doesn't stand alone. We know that only when food, housing, medical care, and economic stability, just to name a few, are secured for all children, is the pump primed to deliver just and equitable schooling. Throughout this book, I will be talking about how *justice is found in the details of teaching and learning*®, while also acknowledging that when all of our societal systems, like the ones referenced above, take an accurate accounting of the racial harm embedded in our national foundation, our efforts at equity can better flourish.

But we don't have time to wait for one or all of these things to be fixed before fixing education. We hope that by attending to the justice in the details of teaching and learning, we can make our sector a model for the other sectors that desperately need transformation.

Justice seekers—people seeking that societal transformation—are not only working to shift their own mindset around what is possible in the world we have. They are also naming injustice and identifying its tangible features so that they can be eliminated and eradicated. We see this happening in the housing sector, as banks begin to acknowledge the financial disparities in communities of color versus white communities and commit to creating products and programs that ignite property ownership opportunities. In education, the acknowledgment of the massive opportunity gap not only has sparked discussion, but has commissioned many federal and state agencies to investigate, gather stakeholders, and create pathways for academic equity.

Justice requires reconciliation, and the path to reconciliation in education requires us to use our skills and identities to acknowledge, name, and unravel the institutional practices that have relegated Black, brown, and Indigenous students to second-class citizenship. Right now, shame about what our nation has done to its most vulnerable peoples has sparked the current wave of book banning and repressive school legislation. Shame tells us to deny harm rather than wrestle with our culpability in it in order to devise a remedy. When we fall victim to shame, we remain at that same level of immobility and reactionary thinking, and never press forward with empathy. Researcher and author Brené Brown often asks us to lean into empathy, connecting to what a person may be feeling without having the same experience, in order to extinguish shame. As humans we are connected within the same ecosystem, and what affects one has an effect on all. As you read this book, I invite you to release the shame that has hampered our progress toward justice for centuries.

Unfortunately, I can't promise you a fix-it manual or a "just tell me how to do it" guide to revolutionizing education. Like you, I am on my own path in figuring all of this out amid national events that are more and more troubling, especially when children and educators are caught in the figurative and literal crossfire of political divides. My own story informs and challenges this work, as yours informs and challenges yours. In some sense, telling my story, examining the highs and lows, and the successes as well as the failures of my professional evolution, has freed me. It has allowed me to take a closer look at myself and the systems I serve. This kind of self- and system analysis are essential when seeking root causes of inequalities and homing in on our spheres of influence.

At best, this book is a journey through the life of one educator who has been both the recipient and conductor of injustices in education and who has grown exponentially in her own equity journey. This book amplifies the lessons I have learned along the way as well as the frameworks those learnings have helped cultivate at UnboundEd. You'll see how I arrived at an understanding of the essential importance of grade-level, engaging, affirming, and meaningful instruction and how that knowledge shapes so many aspects of my work today. My hope is that the book sparks conversations, reconciliation, and hope for future generations of educators and students. My deepest wish is that together we can put the knowledge that *justice is found in the details of teaching and learning*® at the center of our instruction and pedagogy.

1 Educational Inequity: How We Got Here

Years ago, I was sitting in the back of a first-grade classroom, pen and paper at the ready to capture everything I could while observing a teacher in the launch of her new reading block.

I looked around the classroom at the students settling in, and I quickly observed that about one in four children in the class were students of color. With a flick of the teacher's hand, the students began to assemble on the carpet, each one with a whiteboard and a marker. I could tell right away that they were very familiar with this particular routine.

The teacher began the reading block with a read-aloud of *The Three Billy Goats Gruff*. Immediately, when she showed the front cover of the book, a boy with deep brown eyes and black hair called out, "Teacher, teacher, that's a *con dê*! That's a con dê!"

"It is?" the teacher inquired. "Is that how you say 'goat' in Vietnamese?"

"Yes," the same student responded. "My um, um, *bà ngoại* has lots of them!" he announced.

The teacher, not wanting to miss the teachable moment, inquired, "Oh, your bà ngoại . . . Thanh, do you want to tell the rest of our friends what a bà ngoại is?"

He smiled at the chance to teach the class and announced proudly, "That means um, um grandma!"

The teacher started the read-aloud, and I noticed that all the students were leaning in, anticipating the story. When the teacher got to the book's repetitive chorus, "Trip-trap, trip-trap went Billy Goat's hooves as he walked across the bridge," another student—this time a little boy with what looked to be a fresh-cut afro mohawk and a wide smile that showed one tooth missing—proudly repeated the chorus aloud with the teacher. She turned and admonished him with a look. When the teacher got to the chorus again, right in unison with her, the boy chimed in.

This time, the teacher stopped reading and said his name sharply, "Mitchell," and then gave him the signal to be quiet. Mitchell immediately shrugged his shoulders, and his silly grin faded into a pout as his chin dropped down to his chest. He deflated a little bit, sinking into the floor and picking at the carpet to avoid eye contact.

At that moment, for reasons that were not immediately apparent to me, I was drawn to Mitchell. It wasn't as if I hadn't seen that kind of interaction before in my 15 or so years as an educator. Likely, I had even been the initiator of a similar disciplinary exchange. But it was the glimpse of how quickly and palpably Mitchell's demeanor changed, how clearly diminished he became, that caught my attention. I saw in that moment how his light was instantly turned off, and I saw an all-too-familiar feeling that I now can articulate as shame settling in. The shrugging of his shoulders and then the self-soothing behavior of picking at the carpet spurred up an angst in me that, if I was being honest, I hadn't felt since I was in grade school.

I made a note in my journal to circle back with the teacher to discuss the relationship she had with Mitchell and to see if she had noticed the shift in his demeanor following her correction. I was acutely aware that Mitchell's teacher had misinterpreted his outburst as unruliness, rather than as the exercise of a deeply cultural Black practice of choral reading. While she took time to celebrate the cultural and linguistic differences of Thanh, her actions toward Mitchell, just a moment later, had signaled both to him and to the other children that his cultural practices, and by this I mean Black cultural practices, had no place in her lessons.

I glanced at the other students to gauge their reactions to the teacher's reprimand. Had her harshness with Mitchell impacted their own desire to speak up in class? Even in that moment, as I analyzed Mitchell and his classmates, I struggled with an internal argument, to push away what I observed as classroom behavior management, or to lean into the uncomfortable gut feeling of incremental marginalization that laid beneath the teacher's action.

I decided to stay for the entire school day and shadow Mitchell from afar. Several times during the reading block activities, I noticed that Mitchell and his Black and brown classmates who had assembled after the read-aloud in a corner of the classroom, were scolded by the teacher to "watch their noise level," or questioned about whether they were "on track." These were all seemingly normal interactions between a teacher and students, but for me, in this moment, it had moved beyond the standard classroom procedure into a two-way mirror. I was observing Mitchell's adverse reactions to the teacher's constant reprimanding, while simultaneously being reminded of dominant cultural rules of interaction and how they played out, not only in this classroom, but in classrooms across the country. In reprimanding Mitchell during the read-aloud, this teacher had further solidified the disconnect between the cultural language patterns that many students in her classroom were familiar with and "proper" classroom language. Mitchell's cultural language could have been utilized to further all of their learning. What I know now is that this teacher was oblivious to the fact that seemingly minor classroom management actions were conveying a message about whose culture was worthy of being included in instructional practices.

I flashed back to my memories of second grade and that feeling of wanting to sink into the classroom floor, when the teacher had either ignored me or reprimanded me about a rule that I had forgotten or had not even been aware of. I connected to the feeling of shame that I could sense Mitchell was having, that same feeling that had been conveyed to me over and over again as a student maneuvering through classrooms in which I was one of very few students of color, sometimes the only one. In my own education, I had grown accustomed to the persistent shadow of a feeling that I was treated differently because of the color of my skin. When I was young, I simply identified it as "Teacher don't like me." As I grew older, I knew which white teachers tolerated me, which ones despised me, and which ones would physically slink back if I walked up to them. I wondered if I was witnessing the birth of that same shadow in Mitchell.

The expression on Mitchell's face signaled an all-too-familiar surge of humiliation. As a child, encountering a world in which at any moment you are made to feel ashamed or to endure constant reminders that you are discounted, can inflict calluses of sadness that often turn into anger and defiance, or worse, isolation and defeatism. I was also reminded of how those moments led me to my current path: to resolve the explicit and implicit barriers that bias and racism build in our students, ourselves, and the systems in which we serve.

This moment of Mitchell shrinking into himself would resonate even more deeply later in my career, when I read the stats on Black students' disproportionate achievement or the school disciplinary crisis facing Black and brown students.

From Moment to Movement

I had originally been sent to Mitchell's classroom by the suburban school district office where I worked as an early-childhood specialist. In 2005, we wanted to begin preparation for our annual summer professional development (PD) series for elementary teachers. My assignment was to observe a sample of the school's reading blocks, get a sense of how teachers were implementing readers' and writers' workshops, and report back on what possible professional development topics would be pertinent to ensure that the reading blocks were being implemented with fidelity. The district was struggling with an ever-increasing proficiency gap in reading scores, even after overhauling the former expectations of English Language Arts (ELA) instruction and adopting new schedules, curriculum, and support practices.

However, Mitchell's reaction to the teacher that day pushed me into a much broader observation about the small and insidious ways our education system is encoded with deep bias against Black children and other students of color. And when I say "small," I do not mean inconsequential. In fact, it is these ostensibly small interactions, in the details of teaching and learning, that make the biggest difference in the way Black and brown students perceive themselves, how teachers see them, what is expected of them, and their own agency and worth in education and their world beyond.

There are many things one could surmise about what was driving the interactions between Mitchell and his teacher. At first, the exchange seemed to be predicated on discipline; as a teacher early in my career, I would have very quickly validated why there seemed to be such a focus on correcting his behavior. However, having witnessed the patterns of overemphasis on behavioral correction for students of color in various systems, I had a grounded belief as to why Mitchell's teacher was "keeping an eye" on him.

According to research, the overzealous disciplining of Black and brown children in schools plays a significant role in the pathway to low achievement, lack of foundational skills in reading and math, and—the most distressing outcome—incarceration. Black students account for just 15% of all public school students, but they represent about 39% of students suspended from school—an overrepresentation of 23%.[1] In 2014, preschoolers were included in the Civil Rights Data Collection on school discipline, and Black children were found to account for 18% of preschool enrollees and nearly half (48%) of all preschoolers suspended. This disparity contrasted discouragingly with white students, who made up 43% of the preschool population but only 26% of those subject to suspension.[2] When students experience just one standard deviation of a higher suspension rate, their likelihood of being arrested or incarcerated increases by 15% to 20%.[3] The problem of over-disciplining Black children like Mitchell is systemic, and it begins with the smaller interactions I witnessed in this teacher's classroom. However, it also occurred to me that she probably had never considered how her actions fit into larger patterns of over-disciplining Black and brown children.

I was then, and am now, deeply aware of the systematic disenfranchisement that Black, Indigenous, Latinx, and other students of color face in most educational settings, the pressing messages they receive, both implicitly and explicitly, about the value of their non-dominant cultural social norms and communication styles. This awareness is one of the foundational reasons why I went into education in the first place. My hope was, if nothing else, to serve as a small beacon of light to the students of color I encountered on their educational walks. In my eyes, Mitchell's innate, and honestly adorable, urge to respond chorally to the line of repetition the teacher was reading aloud was not distracting or worthy of disciplinary attention.

This was the same reaction I was having in my own head, but I knew enough about social dominant norms not to say it aloud.

After all, choral reading—or call and response—is a part of so many Black cultural spaces I've inhabited in my life. It's a part of church, community rituals, memorials for loved ones, and even movie watching. Augusta Mann explores this important cultural language pattern in her "Touching the Spirit" framework.[4] Touching the Spirit highlights for educators a research-based teaching modality focused on supporting students from the Black and African American cultural background. Mann's work suggests that when we meaningfully incorporate children's cultural practices, we enrich and deepen classroom learning. She is far from alone in these assertions: educational research and recognition of choral response and the devaluation of cultural linguistic differences has existed for decades, along with culturally responsive teaching research from Dr. Gloria Ladson-Billings in the 1990s.[5]

However, like many educators, Mitchell's teacher may not have thought that she could be carrying the legacy of America's educational history in her ideologies about Black students, and about Mitchell in particular. She did not consider that not only does good pedagogy need to be grade-level-appropriate, but that it also has to be engaging, it must affirm children's identities, and it must be meaningful to them. Simply put, this lack of consideration is the outcome of unconscious bias or implicit bias.

Unconscious or implicit bias is the set of automatic and unconscious stereotypes that drive people to behave and make decisions in certain ways. It is the mind's way of making uncontrolled and automatic associations between two concepts very quickly. Much has been said in recent years about implicit bias and its impacts on all aspects of our society, but the most important thing to remember about bias is this: If it is left unchecked, one's lexicon of prejudgments will continue to deepen and drive harmful behavior. We are all bombarded daily with messages from our upbringings, media, and, dare I say, skewed or incomplete understandings of history. Many of these images and messages teach us to simplify, to dismiss, and to ignore the nuances and humanity in the people around us. To counteract these messages—especially as educators—we must continuously and vigilantly interrogate how they are woven throughout our interactions with children and how they inform our academic and behavioral expectations.

Every moment that teachers, administrators, communities, and even families leave their bias unexamined, Black children and other children of color are robbed of their educational freedom. As educators, we must consider how our cultural lenses define liberty both for ourselves and for the students we serve. We will return to the story of Mitchell and his teacher, but to examine our personal biases, first we have to understand where they come from. This begins with understanding the history that brought those biases and presumptions into being and shaped them into what we bring into our classrooms every day.

The Foundation of Bias and the Educational System It Upholds

I've always been struck by the idea of our country's beginnings as the womb of liberty. This metaphorical image of the crucible that is a womb, signals that this country's origins, our national DNA, is a concoction of all the events that led to our nation's founding. This means that the theft of Indigenous tribal land throughout the eighteenth and nineteenth centuries is as much a part of that beginning as the colonists' drafting of their intentions for the colonies of the United States. It means that realities of chattel slavery and vicious slaveholding exist in the legacies of George Washington and Thomas Jefferson, alongside their accomplishments as pioneers of democratic thought.

The word "liberty" signals to me that the colonists, and certainly the drafters of the Declaration of Independence, despite their hypocrisies, knew that the undergirding principle of freedom could not be sacrificed. Our nation's founders and leaders have relied on the strength of this defining purpose to wage wars and bargain treaties for centuries—all in the name of liberty.

Upon close examination, liberty, simply stated, means the power to make choices. History has shown us the value of the choices that liberty affords. The colonists' denial or curtailing of choice was a theft of liberty enacted upon the Indigenous communities as they became victims of the colonial land acquisitions and Manifest Destiny—the audacious, blithe, and violent assumption that colonial expansion was the inevitable entitlement of the colonizers. Choices were taken from the Africans who were violently stolen from their homes and forced to power the economy of this pilfered New World. Centuries later, agency, freedom, and any semblance of home were completely annihilated when the United States government made the audacious decision to create internment camps for Japanese Americans during World War II. I often say that history begets legacies, those legacies have legs, and they walk into our classrooms every day. These foundational choices of our nation are just a few of many steps that take us down the long and winding road leading to the schoolhouse, and to the birth of systemic policies, practices, and procedures that nourish unchecked beliefs about students of color.

Other writers have documented the wider, often ignored, histories in American public schooling today. Depending on educators' own educational backgrounds, some of it may be familiar while other parts are still unknown. But a close look, not only at the beginnings of American systems of subjugation and erasure, but at the foundations that they created in public schooling, is important if we are ever going to work to build a new vision for education.

In the late 1700s, pseudosciences were crafted throughout the Western world to establish the concept of race as a biological fact. Many of the social and biological theories born out of the European "Enlightenment" were used to further entrench the belief that enslaved Africans were of inferior intellect and were unworthy of education. The Enlightenment philosopher John Locke suggested that people of African descent were a subspecies of human because it was believed African women procreated with apes.[7] The Swedish scientist and creator of the modern taxonomy system, Carl Linnaeus, classified Africans as *Homo sapiens afer*, declaring them "sluggish, lazy. . . . [c]rafty, slow, careless. Covered by grease. Ruled by caprice."[6] These ideas continued their legacies across the Atlantic, as scientists like Samuel Morton, the father of American anthropology, declared that the white race had "the highest intellectual endowments" in the human race, allegedly due to the size of their skulls.[7] All of this rhetoric offered fodder not only to further the horrors of slavery, but to extend its legacy far beyond abolition.

For enslaved Africans, whose forced labor powered the economy of the colonies and set this country on its productive economic course, access to the schoolhouse was something systematically and brutally denied. In 1739, a rebellion of enslaved Africans began in South Carolina, and as it swept south to Florida, those rebelling killed 20 enslavers. When the rebellion was ultimately quelled, it ushered in an age of anti-literacy laws.[8] These laws sought to prevent future rebellions and organizing by ensuring that enslaved people caught reading were subjected to a host of punishments, ranging from sale, whippings, removal of their tongues, and death.[9] Thus, by controlling the means to education, the white ruling class sought to moderate the actions and limit the power of enslaved Africans. Even as the Constitution was being conceived and later drafted, enslaved Africans were being actively legislated out of any of the freedoms this vision of liberty—again, the ability to make choices—afforded.

There is more to understand about the degree to which enslavers would go to ensure their enslaved people remained illiterate. Along with terror, through physical violence, slave owners used slave codes to control their human property. These codes were laws used against the enslaved—drafted and enforced based on the idea that enslaved people were not people, but property. Not only did being literate come at the risk of one's life as an enslaved person, those caught *teaching* enslaved Africans how to read could also be subjected to fines or jail time. In Virginia, for instance, the law stated "That if any white person or persons assemble with free negroes or mulattoes . . . for the purpose of instructing such free negroes or mulattoes to read or write, such person or persons shall, on conviction thereof, be fined in a sum not exceeding fifty dollars, and moreover may be imprisoned at the discretion of a jury, not exceeding two months."[10] For enslaved or free persons of color, the penalty was up to 20 lashes.[11]

In the state of Georgia, this happened to Reverend James Simms, who in 1861, was fined by the city of Savannah for teaching enslaved people how to read.[12] Reverend Simms was a free Black man who was repeatedly fined by the city, but he chose fines rather than give up on ensuring his people gained liberty through learning. As previously mentioned, in the 1700s and 1800s, slave codes came to include anti-literacy laws, which continued to rely on legislation to curtail learning opportunities for enslaved people. While enslaved people were allowed to learn "figures," reading was off limits. Since literacy was liberty, then illiteracy was necessary to ensure enslavement.

Abolitionist Frederick Douglass provides a window into understanding the degree to which education was held as a commodity that was used to advance some and restrict others, namely by advancing learning for white citizens while strategically and legislatively ensuring that Black enslaved individuals were forbidden to learn. The formerly enslaved Douglass describes how he came to understand the importance of literacy by overhearing his master, Auld, exclaim to his wife, when he caught her trying to teach Douglass how to read, that Douglass's literacy would only spoil him and make "him unfit to be a slave."[13] Douglass understood that if something as seemingly innocent as sounding out words to read a story could make his master so infuriated and afraid, then that thing must be of great importance.

It is important to recognize that Douglass is a significant part of our national understanding of slave narratives, in part *because* he was able to learn how to read and write. Douglass's story is an anomaly not because he was exceptional in his understanding of the deep importance of reading, but because he did not receive the most extreme punishments many enslaved people suffered when they attempted to usurp their enslavement through literacy. Had he received the punishments many enslaved people did when attempting to write or read, his story too might have been lost to time. Literacy's illegality for enslaved people was not simply a cruel feature of enslavement; it was constructed by white slaveholders and politicians to subvert organizing and insurrection against chattel slavery.

The stories of Douglass and other enslaved people help illuminate how America has arrived at this place of uneven literacy development among groups of students. We learn from Douglass the significance of the power dynamic at play when those who can control the learning of others do so in such a way as to ensure illiteracy for people they do not believe deserve the right to learn. Anti-literacy laws may seem decades, even centuries removed from our current experiences as educators; however, examining these histories affords us an understanding of how the racism and biases that shaped these laws can remorph and reform themselves across time. When we become more attuned to the history of our field, we begin to understand these cycles of implicit bias, and we can use that knowledge to dismantle and end them. We will continue to explore how this history impacts our contemporary understanding of education beyond linguistics and literacy, but first, I want to return to Mitchell's school to illustrate just how fraught that history makes our current communications when we try to confront it in our classrooms and with other educators.

Teaching Mitchell

As I wandered back to the classroom after the students' lunch break, I started playing in my head the conversation that I wanted to have with Mitchell's teacher. I had met her several months prior at a professional development session I had facilitated for the district. She'd approached me after the session, saying she was interested in strengthening her teaching skills in early literacy and very much wanted to support the students in her classroom who were struggling with their literacy development, writing skills, and participation in class. My initial interaction with Mitchell's teacher at that PD session was front of mind after my observation of her classroom later, as I was trying to calculate how to bring up my observation of Mitchell's reaction of shame to her reprimand of his choral reading practice in the classroom.

As we sat down to discuss my observations of her classroom, she was eager to know what I thought of her reading language arts block. Given my knowledge around coaching, I started the "feedback sandwich" with what I had observed that I thought went really well: the students knew the routines, it only took small signals to get their attention, and she had effectively organized her 180-minute reading blocks. The lesson had also been well thought out, with reading centers supporting the students' current grade-level standards.

Then I took a breath, and started the most difficult part of the feedback with a question. "Did you notice the way that Mitchell shifted? And by shifted, I mean Mitchell's demeanor. Did you see how it changed after you reprimanded him for choral reading aloud with you?"

I could tell that the question caught her off guard because she leaned back in her chair, and squinted her eyes as if her vision had suddenly gone out of focus. She responded, "Oh, Mitchell. He's my special little boy." It was her turn to make a feedback sandwich.

She continued: "Yes, sometimes I find it really hard to keep him focused. If I'm honest, he was one of the students I had in mind when I walked up to you at the end of your professional development session. But notice his demeanor? No, he's my chatty kid, the student for whom I'm always having to bring his attention back to the class."

I listened as she unfurled the reasons why she had responded as she had. I took it in as she gave background on her relationship with Mitchell. I really tried to listen to understand and push down my own assumptions. But what I was really pushing down was my "spidey sense" of encountering biases as a person of color. I was really pushing down the frustrations I had been accustomed to ignoring for many years.

When she was finished, I spoke. I explained how observing Mitchell's reaction to her seemingly simple disciplinary action, caused me to pause and to not only notice the shame he experienced but the triggering effect it had on me. I shared that these interactions between her and Mitchell had awakened a revelation. Perhaps it was the culminating years of having taught first grade myself, then becoming a literacy coach, or maybe it was my many years of training leaders in creating equitable environments for all students that was fueling our conversation. But for the first time, on this critical point, I saw clearly. The reality was that what I had originally seen as a phenomenon of Black and brown students' engagement in classrooms, was actually a failure of cultural awareness and the influence of deep bias in teaching. I saw how these interactions had even impacted my own navigation of school as a Black student.

I listened intently to Mitchell's teacher's protests and asked her if I could offer up a different perspective of the dynamics between her and Mitchell. I provided her with the definition of implicit bias and described how all of us are victims of racism's smog. We inhale it on a daily basis through images, media, and the layers of who we are. Family dynamics, religious perspectives, political affiliations, and experiences inside and outside of our immediate communities all shape the bias we bring into our classrooms.

She shared with me that she didn't agree with my assessment of bias, because she didn't see color. She further explained: "If someone were to ask me about the race of my students I would really have to stop and consider each child individually and tally up my considerations. Is that being 'color blind' or is it simply looking at students as individuals with individual learning challenges?"

Again, I sat there pushing down my own bias alarm and asked her permission to challenge her thinking. I began by reading back to her my observation notes, specifically the part where Thanh offered up his story about his bà ngoại having goats. I read aloud her response and the encouragement she gave Thanh in the moment: to not only share with the class, but to teach his classmates what the word "bà ngoại" meant. I told her that at that moment she used Thanh's cultural tools to support the teaching and understanding of the text. I then read her my observation notes when Mitchell began to chorally read aloud with her. I asked her if she was familiar with the cultural context from which Mitchell used the unwritten cultural norm to join in chorally with a repeated text. I gave her examples of how it's used in some Black churches, civic meetings, and in homes. I asked her if she considered his reading aloud chorally in a cultural context.

She sat quietly for a moment and then stated, "I don't think I ever considered African-Americans as having a culture. I just assumed my cultural context was theirs. I mean they don't speak another language and I guess I assumed culture was a specific language and traditions of culture from a specific region in the world. From what I understand, African-Americans don't have any of that."

And in just a few short sentences, she had unearthed her own bias and excavated an assumption that is at the heart of much of American education: that Black children do not have culture, only pathology. Because of her unconscious bias, Mitchell's actions could not be evaluated in the same cultural context as Thanh's. America's educational DNA ensured that his joyful choral response could only be coded as misbehavior and unruliness.

Whether or not we know it, there is cultural DNA encoded throughout the American education system, built upon the foundational beliefs about Black people's educability—or lack thereof. To varying degrees, this encoded anti-Blackness and white centricity also impacts our views about the intelligence of Indigenous, Latinx, and other children of color. We often do not learn these histories of how this belief came to be. However, our lack of awareness does not negate the reality that we are also governed by the subtleties of this belief system flowing through the DNA of our educational system and even ourselves. Such ideological DNA has shaped laws, policies, and practices, which in turn have yielded the disparate and inequitable outcomes that we have become accustomed to, take for granted as absolute, and continue to exacerbate today.

Denaturing Our DNA

Inequity is *core* to American education, simply because our educational system was built with inequity and cultural theft encoded in its DNA. Knowing this helps us understand why, despite endless decades of education reform, America's education system remains egregiously inequitable, with predictable student outcomes that fall along established societal fault lines. As we consider an authentic, lasting way out of these entrenched, accepted educational inequities, there must be a real discussion to unwind the racialized encoding that got us here.

As a nation, we have been led to believe that school is the great equalizer, that it provides equal avenues for all children to advance in our society. Unfortunately, data and centuries of lived experience have shown us school is anything but that great equalizer.[14] While the

history of slavery and anti-literacy laws are foundational to racial
inequity in education, there is more to learn about how we "got here."
To fully understand, we have to explore the conditions that allowed
those historical anti-literacy laws to morph and compound in the
century and a half since enslavement. We must spend some time
decoding the underpinnings of our education system so we can see
our way forward to creating and ensuring that education becomes the
equalizer every student deserves. We have to see how the details of
educational injustice began, so that we can get to the details of its
opposite: truly just teaching and learning.

Unfortunately, navigating classroom settings that are so deeply
steeped in unconscious bias requires Black students and many
students of color to internalize the dominant cultural norms. In order
to survive in school, they must tuck away who they are, their home
language, their ways of communicating, the working norms of their
communities, and rules of engagement. For students of color, this
forced disconnection is compounded over and over again, in
classroom after classroom, school after school, year after year.
Coupled with other explicit messages that tell Black and brown
children that certain subjects or opportunities are not designed for
them, our educational system, more often than not, constructs a
pipeline of exclusion and harm.

Some students of color, like myself, got the home lessons of "how
to conduct themselves in public." And by that, my mother *actually*
meant "around white people." Some friends and colleagues have
shared with me that there was no home lesson about this type of
cultural assimilation. Thus, they found themselves learning lessons in
their day-to-day interactions with teachers and other adults in the
building. But for every student, including Mitchell, family and
community culture does not drop off when they enter their school
buildings. More importantly, it precedes them with every action they
initiate. Mitchell will continue to exhibit behaviors and functions

grounded in his culture. As educators, it is our job to build classrooms in which Mitchell's culture is celebrated and not penalized.

So . . . how do we get past the structures that continue to hold so many Black and brown students back? How do we move past the current education model that centers white cultures as normative and all other cultures as outside of that acceptable norm? How do we instead design something that allows Black and brown students to be their fully realized selves, with educators who've chosen to engage in work whose purpose is to build students up instead of erasing them, their languages, and their cultures?

As simple as it sounds, we have to make a collective decision to do so. We need to make a decision that what we *say* we believe gets enacted in real time, in real ways, with real students. Of course, this sounds simple enough, yet the historical data, which continues into the present despite decades of reforms that were ostensibly equity-minded and driven, tells a different story. At UnboundEd, we have received countless requests for information about "how to teach Black children," other children of color, and children of different languages and dialects; these inquiries seem like they will never end. In 1897, W.E.B. DuBois discussed the question posed around his existence as a Black man in America; he wrote that underlying his every interaction with non-Black people was the persistent question "How does it feel to be a problem?" Over 120 years later, the question of "how to teach Black children" continues this pathologizing. We continue to struggle to address the learning needs of students who seemingly "deviate"[15] from the dominant norm, without interrogating the norms we now know to be encoded with the same DNA as slave codes and anti-literacy laws.

Such norms have created a racialized caste system in America. In this caste system, those who do not hold the "correct" racial identity, experience compounded negative economic and political outcomes throughout their lives. The reality is that in order to support a fabricated racial caste system, the land holders and politicians who helped forge our nation's founding identity simultaneously enshrined racism and anti-Blackness, and forced illiteracy into law. The cognitive dissonance of that truth is one we must grapple with, both as a nation and as educators who have actively chosen to be in this marvelous field.

To upend the legacy of relegating Black people to the educational margins, we must also own our underlying beliefs and understand how those beliefs shape the advancement of what we ask our students to consume as materials worth learning. We know that historically Black students (as well as Indigenous, Latinx, and other students) have not had equitable access to an education that is on grade-level, engages their minds, affirms their identities, or is meaningful to them. The question now becomes, how do we look this history in the face, understand what it has meant for groups of people, and strategically once and for all create a new DNA line to leave a legacy of equity and academic achievement for all students?

Often educators ask me for something more concrete to use in their classrooms to work toward the goals they have for their students and themselves in racial equity work. Too often educators receive the message to "fix this" or "fix that" in making their classrooms equitable and safe places for children to learn, without ever being given the tools to do so. This is one of the reasons why UnboundEd will provide access to our Anti-Bias toolkit (you can find the link at the end of this book), and why I will be referencing its tools throughout. In this way, educators can access our foundational professional development lessons to bring our ideas into practice in classrooms.

As we move through this book, you will work through these historical legacies and explore ways to create a new DNA lineage to reshape your legacy toward a more just education. You will help unearth the cognitive dissonance that those who are attempting to disrupt systems of power must grapple with. You will examine the details of your teaching and learning to better understand where you've been and where you are now, so that you can move forward. You will more clearly evidence your beliefs in the intellectual capacity of every child you have the opportunity to teach and unwind the long road of inequity to which you might have inadvertently been contributing.

2 Witnessing and Signifying: How Lenses Shape Our Teaching

In some respects, the moment of witnessing—I mean really seeing—Mitchell's reaction and identifying it as a moment of inflicted shame, sits with me to this day. It ignited within me what my grandmother used to call "the signifying." I needed to share with Mitchell's teacher what I believed was missing: that she had to combine literacy instruction with her awareness of the bias at play in the discretionary spaces of the teaching and learning in the classroom. Signifying is an indication that a fundamental change in thinking or philosophy is happening. It is also a Black American colloquialism that can mean "I'm insulting you while also showing affection." In this instance, it felt as though I needed to signify in the Black American colloquialism tradition, that I knew a "courageous conversation," as defined by Glenn Singleton, was necessary.

Neither I nor Mitchell's teacher would leave the conversation comfortable, but it was necessary to raise her awareness that perhaps her beliefs were driving the expectations of learning and or

behavior—and could be earmarked with implicit messages that were
pushing her actions toward Mitchell and other students of color—in
her classroom. I was able to confirm some of the teacher's implicit
bias when we met to discuss the lesson.

After that first observation, I inquired about her background as a
teacher and what led her to Mitchell's school. She began by telling
me, "I chose to come to this school because I wanted to help students
like Mitchell. I knew that the students in this school came from a
high-poverty background and that the school was struggling with
academic achievement. And I wanted to make a difference." She
continued to insist, "I don't see color. I view all my students the same.
I just want Mitchell and his classmates to be good citizens and good
students. Mitchell, like many of his classmates, struggles with grade-
level work and needs a lot of attention. I am in constant search for
the right approach or strategy to keep Mitchell engaged so that he
does not become a distraction for his other classmates."

I began to wonder as she shared her thinking with me. Why were
the alarms going off in my head again, and why were they resonating
not only with the shame I was witnessing in Mitchell's experience, but
with me as a Black educator? Some of the concerns I could put into
words, such as the color blindness she named and the deficit language
she was using to describe Mitchell and his classmates of color. Yet,
there was also an innate feeling that was almost unnameable, an
"othering" that I was also sensing. As a Black educator, I've noticed
many moments like this in my career, when something feels off, but
I haven't always had the tools, language, or even the permission to
name the discordant feeling in the moment. Mitchell's teacher was
describing her reason for wanting to teach at this particular school to
work with high-poverty students when, according to the school data,
the student body was actually a mix of low- *and* middle-income
households. And the academic struggle she named was also evident
even in the district's *highest* socioeconomic neighborhoods, where

students and parents had access to resources and tutoring outside of school.

In fact, the district recognized its disparaging data around English Language Arts (ELA) in the ways *all* students were being affected, which was why I was visiting her school that day. I often say that if a school system has the academic flu, then the students of color are experiencing pneumonia. They are impacted like their white or affluent peers, but are often given inadequate opportunities to catch up. And so, the students of color and English language learners were acutely affected by the entire district's low literacy and writing skills. The district at large, in efforts to raise the ELA and writing achievement for all students, was switching the ELA curriculum, and the teachers in this school didn't yet have sufficient knowledge to teach the new ELA model.

When I debunked her assumptions and asked where she'd heard the incorrect narrative about her school, she answered, "We all assume these facts in this building." It was clear to me that despite her claims at colorblindness, the race of the school's students had impacted her assumptions about who they were and which households they came from. I inquired further about her colorblind lens; I asked her to tell me more about her thinking behind "not seeing color." She explained that she was raised to believe it was taboo to discuss someone's ethnicity and that we were all a part of the melting pot of this country. In an effort to challenge this particular line of thought, I started talking to her about the research I was reading from various authors and scholars like Dr. Gloria Ladson-Billings and Dr. Beverly Tatum, on how to recognize the ways in which implicit and explicit bias shows up in teaching and learning. I explained the indignity toll: that is, that teaching without a lens of equity takes a daily toll on the academic and self identities of students of color. I explained that this purported and unexamined colorblindness could further these inequities and indignities.

What I couldn't articulate in my early career track as a teacher was that whenever I observed environments where students of color were present, I noticed the ways that implicit bias may have been at play in their learning and school environments. For instance, bias is obvious to me in school hallways in which children are walking single file, with bubbles in their mouths, to prevent them from talking to each other. This ill-advised classroom management strategy asks kids to close their lips and puff their cheeks, as if they are holding a bubble. These are practices and structures that don't increase learning, but instead induct primarily students of color into a carceral mindset that their white and affluent peers rarely, if ever, experience. Silence directives in hallways and other exclusionary disciplinary policies in schools disproportionately impact and target Black children. This is both an outgrowth of the white dominant society, and a specific action toward Black children that has its roots in slavery and the systematic control of Black people's bodies and free movement. It's why terms like "willful defiance" are leveraged against Black children more than white children.

I've also seen how bias influences learning content that holds a single view or perspective, without ever considering how it may land on the ears of students from Black, Indigenous, or other communities—those who rarely see themselves reflected in stories, nonfiction topics, or depictions of "influential" figures in science, math, and social studies.

Mitchell's shame and the teacher's named desire to search for the "right" strategy to thwart his behavior is now with me when I observe a teacher executing a lesson to a majority class of Black and brown students. One of these strategies is rooted in low expectations. I notice teachers skipping over rigorous questions and activities, only to insert questions or texts that are grade levels below students' abilities and what they deserve, in part because I understand that bias informs that choice. Because of bias, educators do not question their own intentions in "meeting students" at their assumed level of intelligence and abilities. Our inherent belief about students and what they can do is connected to the shame we inadvertently project onto our students. We may leave unquestioned students' lack of skill sets of unfinished learning—that is, concepts students have not yet mastered—knowledge they will need to grasp upcoming ideas. In other words, when our own unexamined expectations are low, we may not question a lack of skill sets as anything out of the ordinary. Teachers can address unfinished learning by re-engaging with concepts their students haven't grasped *within* their grade-level expectations, focusing on how to eliminate students' shame instead of systemizing it through remedial coursework. And yet, bias forecloses this approach in many classrooms and schools.

For example, I once witnessed the immediate effects of biased thinking around expectations of learning while walking to a classroom in a well-known charter school, housed in a historic Louisiana building. Inside, I immediately took stock of the school's predominantly Black student population and overwhelmingly white teaching and leadership staff. I then sat in on a fifth-grade math lesson and walked around the room to peek in on the students working on their assignment: a self-paced computer program that asked them to figure out pictorial addition sums. Any educator could glean that this lesson was meant for a kindergarten or first-grade lesson, not children on their way to middle school.

A young girl with brown skin and beautiful, intricate braids grabbed my arm to stop my progress down the aisle. She pulled me down to whisper, "Can you be our teacher?" As I rose and made eye contact with her, I saw a pleading in her eyes. Looking around the room, I realized that what I initially thought was students' over-compliance in this silent math classroom, was truly catatonic boredom. I still feel the rock in my throat when I think about that moment, the look in her eyes that showed more than her risk of being called out for not focusing. It was a plea of wanting to be removed from the purgatory of stiflingly low learning expectations and from the presumptions that were most certainly being made in that moment and in many moments to come.

What drove the teachers and leaders at that school to live down to their expectations of students' intellectual capability to 40 minutes of rote, below-grade-level basic math facts and activities?

I pulled the teacher aside and asked, "What is the goal of this activity?"

She responded, "Well, these children have severe discipline issues, and many of them only know a miniscule amount of math facts. I can't possibly teach them fifth-grade content if they can't add."

I was not able to reconcile this narrative with what I had seen previously in classrooms in which students with identified and documented behavioral needs were held to higher expectations and given much more rigorous work. I glanced around the room, in which I could hear a pin drop, and I tried to associate their current behavior with what I had experienced in students who struggled with traditional classroom management practices. There was simply no comparison. Not only could her students do far more, but the mind-numbing environment was clearly doing damage. In fact it was inhumane.

I went back to the school leader to inquire further. "I didn't realize this was a self-contained classroom."

She quickly responded with a look of confusion, "It's not."

Not wanting her to think I was making assumptions, I responded, "Well the classroom teacher just informed me that the students in this classroom (all 34 of them) had severe disciplinary issues."

Her response came after a nervous giggle. "Oh, she is new to teaching and has had some struggles with her classroom management.

She has received coaching and was told to ensure that she kept the students on task and rewarded them when they have complied."
I very quickly got to see what the reward was, because the timer went off and the teacher turned on a classroom speaker that blasted the latest hip hop song. The students bopped their heads and mouthed the words in their seats. Once again, it was clear that unexamined bias fueled these learning practices and would ultimately contribute to patterns of unfinished learning for that young girl and her classmates. Unfortunately, in that role, I never had the opportunity to follow up with that teacher to share my observations and concerns. But when I see classroom practices like this repeated and watch them develop into patterns that impact Black and brown students, I have moments of anguish.

I would be remiss if I only accounted for times of witnessing educational injustice as an outside observer, without confessing my own participation in supporting and *creating* similar structures with the children of color I've taught or guided as a school leader. Early on in my career, I desperately wanted to succeed as a "good teacher"—so much so that I never questioned the structures or rules of engagement set by my school or our school system. In fact, I thought my role was to stand as an example to my students of a Black woman who had "beaten the odds" and to encourage them to play the game, so they too could beat the same odds I had battled some 20 years earlier.

As a teacher and later an administrator, I frequently went right into the "how to fix" the students of color, and I never stopped to consider why they "needed fixing" in the first place. I supported the enactment of remediation or structures of discipline that mimicked penal systems, and I often sat frustrated about why "these kids" wouldn't do right. Just like Mitchell's teacher, I assigned labels to justify why I reacted and/or enacted certain rules and regulations. Like that fifth-grade math teacher, I never fully considered the role of implicit bias and its impact on my beliefs about the students and

communities I was serving—even when those students looked
like me.

Other educators of color, our white colleagues, and I used deficit
reasoning and thinking without reflection. We told ourselves,
sometimes out loud, that lowering expectations for learning was
building confidence in the students who were sent to us with such
great deficits. I cannot count how many reading programs and math
remedial pull-outs and after school programs I sanctioned that either
dressed up as "edutainment" moments for students or were disguised
as acceleration efforts. My colleague at UnboundEd, Alice Wiggins,
uses this term to describe the lengths we as educators will sometimes
go to create shortcuts in learning. Edutainment is when we try to trick
the kids into being educated while being entertained at the same time,
instead of making the learning inherently engaging by inviting
students to be their whole selves and asking them what is fulfilling to
them. We here at UnboundEd lean on GLEAM™ instruction—grade-
level, engaging, affirming, and meaningful—which is a counterbalance
to the gimmicks of edutainment.

As a middle school leader, I spent so much time, on a daily basis,
focusing on what the students didn't have that I grew weary of trying
to dismantle what I thought were the barriers to their learning. If a
student was an assigned seventh grader and read on a third-grade
level, I immediately went into remediation mode, working with
teachers to restructure entire classes so that the student could "read at
their level." I paid very little attention to how many hours and days
the students spent outside of their grade-level work. I didn't have the
time to learn the researched and evaluated skills and pedagogies that
are essential in accelerating student learning.

Like many educators who came of age in the era of education
reform of the 1990s through the late 2010s, I focused heavily on
aesthetics, giving students the appearance of the structure I assumed
they were lacking. As a teacher and later a school leader, I wanted the

students to dress as if they were in a building of high academia: uniforms, ties, and all. But once they sat at their desks, the expectations of high academia were placed on a shelf, except for the students who demonstrated assimilated cultural norms or who read on grade level and beyond. I didn't push their teachers to distinguish between designing scaffolding strategies that led students toward more complex material, instead of remediating to the point that students did not grow academically. I didn't push the district to bring in materials that were structured with rigor in mind. I was a cog in the wheel of a machine that was grinding children down—especially Black and brown children—and stripping them of their educational agency, intrapersonal growth, and belief in who they were and what they were capable of. We as educators are in the "thinking business"; we must continue to nourish our craft. If we demand that our students engage in productive struggle in learning, then we too have to continue to grow our knowledge, skill sets, and critical thinking.

Oftentimes, years later, I would meet the "fruits of our labor" out in the community: students who had matriculated out of our halls and were adulting as best as they could. My former students sometimes worked at the mall or in restaurants I frequented. I was always elated to see them, all grown up, but I would immediately be met with guilt that their dreams of big careers or expansive lifestyles were less attainable because of the education they received with us. In fact, making it out of poverty was nearly unattainable, in part because my fellow educators and I did not teach young people the foundational skills necessary to thrive or to support their desired life trajectories. The aesthetics we created around discipline and rigor did little to help them to fill out a FAFSA application, enroll in a college, or matriculate into careers that would provide financial security. We had not equipped them to be the kind of students that other students like them needed to see in the future. We had neglected to do all of this, but also I, as a Black woman educator, had unknowingly contributed to solidifying their place in cyclical and systemic poverty.

While I often sensed that something was wrong in our approach, the reasons for this would take years for me to unravel. To even discover the humane and more effective ways to educate our Black and brown students—an alternative to the ways my colleagues and I had offered—I had to know more about the system in which I was working. I have come to believe that if we educators want to push our practice into something that is truly worthy of our students, we have to first deeply engage with the historical foundation that we still uphold today in our school systems. Why? Because the type of K–12 education many students of color receive today—an education that places limits on their aspirations—is inextricably linked with how education for Black and brown students has developed historically in America, and how that development shapes the lenses and layers we bring to our work. To understand this link more fully, let's continue our exploration of the American education system, including this country's denial of liberty by denying education.

The Reconstruction of Education

I have sat in my era of Maya Angelou's most poignant (and, might I add, overused and often appropriated) life norm, "Do the best you can until you know better. Then when you know better, do better." What many of us don't talk about as educators, is that knowing better can very well carry shame. Every act of assimilation, discipline, and overcorrection of children's behavior, I truly did out of love for my students. However, that show of love was predicated on their compliance and assimilation. They were successful only if they followed the assimilated systems I erected based on my own experience in school, straight out of my "this is how I made it" rule book. I wanted them to get further along the trajectory than I was, as long as they were prepared for career, college, or beyond. But the critical question was: according to whose measures and defined expectations?

What I didn't fully understand early in my career was that I was functioning within a system of institutional racism, which was deeply codependent with the more macro reality of structural racism. Institutional racism is the blocking of resources, power, and opportunity to discriminate against people of color. Whereas structural racism is a system in which policies, institutional practices, cultural representations, and other norms work in various, often reinforcing ways to perpetuate racial group inequity. Structural racism is not something a few people or institutions choose to practice. Instead, it has been a feature of the social, economic, and political systems in which we all exist. I often compare institutional and systemic racism to how classical music works. You have your institutions (the schools and classrooms I led, housing inequity for Black people, or health disparities for Indigenous communities) that function like sections (strings, wood instruments, wind instruments, etc.), which all coordinate and are conducted to function as an orchestra, a cohesive system. As I was attempting to navigate my students through assimilationist hoops, I was missing the sounds of this philharmonic orchestra of inequity.

The messages that drove my beliefs about how Black and brown students learn and should behave were based on my own experience as a product of institutional and structural racism. As a first-time teacher, I was given the keys to my classroom, an enthusiastic "We'll see you at evaluation time," and very little else in terms of pedagogical or practical support. As a Black educator, I faced additional pressure to get the students of color to "act right" or be "motivated to learn" by using my cultural passport to persuade them. I was incentivized to believe there was only one way to attain academic progress, because I had just 180 days to ensure that my students were equipped to take on the next grade level. This entire cauldron of pressure never allowed me to stop and ask pertinent questions like: What norms of learning, other than meritocracy, can I use in my classroom? How can I support students in grade-level work while scaffolding and building for unfinished learning? What cultural realities are being considered in classroom norms of engagement, collectivism, expectations of work, usage of language variants, native language, and/or home language? These are the types of questions we ask as educators seeking to deliver instruction that is grade-level, engaging, affirming, and meaningful. If we are teaching assimilation for our students' own benefit to excel in school and life, why aren't we being explicit about that?

It wasn't until I started closely examining the historical arc of education for Black and brown students that I really began to understand where the notions of assimilation were bred and how I was rewarded for being the "Black unicorn" in many of my school settings. Before, I never questioned my place as the rare Black student that somehow made it to the honors track. But the process of digging deep into the morphing and re-morphing of our education system—into its current state, unearthing its persistent and systemic racist policies, practices, and procedures—shifted my understanding of why I had enacted such assimilationist classroom ideals. And, honestly, that deeper understanding has lifted much of my shame.

Often when I hear discussions of the evolution of our national education system, the conversation is limited. As a collective, we focus on the losses and lack that racism constructed for Black, Indigenous, and Latinx Americans, a fact that, when coupled with white supremacy, allows us to believe that Black and brown people themselves are somehow lacking. For example, in general, the national discourse around desegregation, particularly with regard to education, is that Black and brown children suffered under the separation from white communities. This thread of discourse tells us that the civil rights era cases of *Brown v. Board of Education* created a means for integration and legally dismantled "separate but equal." The cases, we are taught, were a net win for Black and brown children, schools, and communities.

However, a huge moment of transformation in my career came when I realized that this narrative only serves to reinforce the idea that Black, Indigenous, and Latinx communities are inherently under-resourced and ill-equipped to teach their own children. And while the desegregation cases did attack the myriad legal hurdles that kept Black and brown schools from accessing the resources their students desperately needed, the truth of segregated schooling was much more nuanced. What is frequently left unexplored is the period *between* the two historical epochs of enslavement and Jim Crow, or *before* the forced assimilation of Indigenous children into residential schools.

We rarely learn how formerly enslaved Black people in America were able to construct lives, education, business, and thriving communities for themselves post-slavery in the time of Reconstruction, or about the robust, intergenerational learning spaces that were prized in Black communities, and, for that matter, their Latinx and Indigenous counterparts. My colleague Brandon White, our resident historian at UnboundEd and creator of our podcast series *The Complexion of Teaching and Learning*, has worked internally to teach us the rich history of what those communities of color were actually experiencing as they thrived in many ways, even when they lacked resources. From his teachings I have received a fuller picture of how Black and brown communities have pushed, and still are pushing, for an equitable and equalized education.

In many ways, the end of legal enslavement meant the shattering of the American nation as it had previously existed, both in its days as a collection of colonies and later as an aspiring free republic. In this new era, the country's main economic engine—which powered not only the slave states, but also those that banned slavery—was effectively illegal. Alongside a new nation, a new national understanding needed to be reconstructed.

For the formerly enslaved, not a second of this moment of rebuilding and recreation was wasted. In the days, months, and years immediately following the Emancipation Proclamation, freed Black Americans set about the task of defining freedom for themselves, their children, and their communities. In the sphere of education, freed Black Americans aimed to right the wrongs of centuries of forced illiteracy and intellectual subjugation. Freed Black people understood their ability to remain free rested in their ability to become literate and create a widely literate Black society.

Despite severely limited resources, freed Black Americans established schools without government or philanthropic help. During Reconstruction, the General Superintendent of Schools for the Freedmen's Bureau was John W. Alvord, a white clergyman, whose job was to observe and identify needs to support newly freed people, stated: "[Negroes] often say we want to show how much we can do ourselves, if you will only give us a chance." He also noted the resourcefulness they exercised, citing "Some young man, some woman, or old preacher, in cellar, or shed, or corner of a Negro meeting-house, with the alphabet in hand, or a torn spelling book, is their teacher."[1] During the beginning of Reconstruction, these freed schools were often funded, built, and taught by Black Americans themselves and since "communal literacy" was a traditional value in many African cultures, these new schools were often places for freed Black children and adults alike.[2] Elijah Marrs, a Black Civil War veteran who moved back to Kentucky and taught at a school financially maintained by Black trustees, was one of many freedmen who saw teaching literacy as a civic and communal duty.[3] It was those same communal literacy practices that I witnessed when I saw Mitchell trying so fervently to enact through choral reading with his teacher, which he no doubt picked up from his home life or church.

Across the South, directly following emancipation, African-Americans established schools and the rise of freed Blacks who made education their priority became the catalyst for poor whites to begin finding ways to educate their children. As Heather Andrea Williams explains in her book, *Self-Taught: African American Education in Slavery and Freedom*, "The continuing and expanding interest in education was certainly not lost on southern whites who understood the implications of black people's continued pursuit of formal education."[4] From emancipation to 1870, these Freedmen's schools would increase the school attendance rate by 100% in some counties and drive the literacy rate up by 40% in some counties.[5]

While the self-determination for education was strong within freed Black communities, access to resources could not keep pace with the drive to learn and teach. Beginning in 1865, African-American educators and students slowly began connecting with the American Missionary Association (AMA) for resource assistance. While helpful in providing more of the training, staff capacity, supplies, and funding denied to Black schools because of racist efforts led by state and local governments, the AMA's invitation into the work of Freedmen's schools partially led to a colonization of Black education. The AMA routinely hired white female teachers over Black ones, and sent the most trained Black teachers to "undesirable locations." These decisions weren't made with the needs of struggling students in mind, but instead to cater to the comfort of white staff.[6]

Even though white educator recruits were often valued over Black educator recruits, on average Black teachers stayed teaching longer in the South than did white teachers. According to the AMA's own data, Black teachers averaged 2.25 terms, while white teachers averaged 1.95 terms.[7] This is a trend we see echoed in schooling today, where Black educators are undervalued and under-resourced relative to their white peers. The majority of modern teacher preparation programs have not remedied this problem and, one could argue, are still being largely formulated by the AMA's missionary-style programming.

Battling White Discontent

Even with missionary assistance, Black people pursuing education
during Reconstruction were met with varying degrees of violence.
All across the South, as Black people strove for education, white
southerners, in their demand for a subservient Black underclass,
became determined to undermine these newly freed Black people's
ability to educate their children. Their worry was that once formerly
enslaved people got a taste of being educated, they would "soon be
thundering at the gates of our Universities."[8] Alvord noted: "The
educational work in Maryland has had such opposition, such as
stoning children and teachers at Easton, rough handling and
blackening the teacher at Cambridge." He also observed, "Colored
churches have been burned in Cecil, Queen Ann, and Somerset
counties, to prevent schools being opened in them, all showing that
negro hate is not by any means confined to the low south."[9]

While general harassment and threats toward white educators
were common, Black people involved in the effort to provide and
receive an education were often subject to shootings, whippings, and
even murder. School teachers were attacked, had their property
destroyed, and dealt with assassination, in a climate none too
different from what civil rights activists would encounter some one
hundred years later.[10] Elijah Marrs himself, a veteran turned
schoolteacher in Tennessee, was terrorized by angry white citizens
who shot their guns at the school while kids were playing outside of
it. This white discontent with Black-led or even Black-centered
educational practices reverberates through our current time, as
teachers of all races today are facing termination for displaying Black
Lives Matters signs in their classrooms or teaching about our
country's full history and its ever-turning tides of racial injustice.
Teaching about how that injustice fuels today's legislation is enough
to get educators fired. These various legislations are a rebirth of old
tactics used historically to fear-monger and to stop not only students

of color, but all students, from obtaining knowledge, understanding, and, dare I say, empathy for those facing the most disenfranchisement in our society. In a nation founded upon the creed that all men are created equal, it stands to reason that examining the record of our sins, setbacks, and failures as well as our virtues, triumphs, and successes is the only pathway to creating that equality. And instead of fostering learning communities equipped to correct our wrongs as a nation, the current legislation frames the natural discomfort inherent to learning and changing as detrimental to white children.

Anger, fear, and jealousy of Black education not only led to terrorism from white citizens after the Civil War, but it, ironically, also led to education advocacy for white students as well. Historically, because the county populations were vastly spread out and there was political opposition to taxes, Southern schools did not have the same sturdy common school system as the North.[11] However, as Williams details in *Self-Taught: African-American Education in Slavery and Freedom*—an account of how white rage led to the demise of Black schools, particularly in the South—"Despite the fact that education was not an enumerated right, African-Americans continued to publicly claim it."[12]

The fear of being outpaced by the advocacy and resilience of Black educators and students in the South, prompted poor white southerners to advocate and build their own educational institutions during Reconstruction. There were even cases in which white parents sent their children to these traditionally Black schools because there wasn't a traditional school system to send them to and because the instruction was high quality.[13] While the image of the impoverished and failing Black schools necessarily animated the discourse around *Brown v. Board*, our knowledge of this time paints a more complex picture of a series of thriving Black schools facing both a legislated lack of resources and localized white violence.

Colonization in Black and Indigenous Schooling

The pursuit of education during Reconstruction went from
independently established schools, to Freedmen's schools, to common
school systems, and then colleges, which included Historically Black
Colleges and Universities (HBCUs). Black colleges and universities
arose in full force starting in the late 1800s. They would produce the
first "formally" trained Black teachers in the South.[14] While the
addition of colleges and universities to the continuum of Black
American education was momentous, it was not without serious and
concerning ramifications. During the inauguration of HBCUs, the
influence of white-backed funding and leadership had a significant
impact on what goals colleges and universities set with regard to
educating Black men and women.

As a graduate of an HBCU, Florida A&M University, I learned
first-hand about the initial support and the intent behind building a
"workforce" suitable to their interests. HBCUs and many formidable
educational leaders in the Black community rose against those interests
and lobbied on behalf of the intellectual and liberation aspirations of
many Black people in the United States. Instead of providing education
with the goal of unlocking the full power of the Black community,
HBCUs were invested in developing a controlled, semi-skilled working
class. General Samuel Armstrong, founder and instructional theorist for
the model HBCU, Hampton University (then called Hampton
Institute), noted the need for a specifically Black labor force for the
South. "There is no source whatever of a suitable supply in lieu of Negro
labor. The large, low swampy, malarial, but highly productive area of the
South would become almost a desert without it. The successful
Southern farmer knows that he has the best labor in the world. The
Negro is important to the country's prosperity."[15]

Armstrong envisioned Hampton Institute as a school-to-labor
pipeline, with Black teachers guiding the process. He noted in
the mission statement he drafted for Hampton, "The thing to

be done . . . is clear: to train selected Negro youths who shall go out and teach and lead their people . . . to teach respect for labor; to replace stupid drudgery with skilled hands; and in this way build up an industrial system for the sake, not only of self-support and intelligent labor, but for the sake of character."[16] He went even further, stating: "The darkies are so full of human nature and have to be most carefully watched over. To simply control them is one thing, but to educate, to draw them out, to develop the germ of good possibilities into firm fruition, requires the utmost care."[17] This kind of surveillance pedagogy—which managed to infiltrate even the hallowed halls of schools explicitly dedicated to the growth of Black Americans—is echoed in the lined hallways of many schools serving Black and brown children today. Unfortunately, this attitude is not "in the past"; it is what I saw in Mitchell's classroom and in so many other schools in which I have both worked and observed.

It was not until I read more of the research on educational history and listened to colleagues like Brandon that I began to articulate the gut-level knowledge I had intuited from seeing Mitchell and other students over the course of my career. Simply put, students who are both shamed and framed as the below-grade-level "other" are defined against a standard that is institutionally, and in practice, culturally sanctioned as the right—and therefore most assimilated to whiteness—way to educate.

Despite this covert control over the academic, economic, and psychological trajectory of HBCUs exerted by Armstrong and others, Heather Andrea Williams writes that their educational practices didn't always have the final say. They could not fully eliminate the passion, power, and purpose of Black educators, nor could they limit their pursuit of a truly liberatory education on behalf of Black Americans at HBCUs.[18] Like many forward-thinking Black teachers of today, these Black educational pioneers had to use creative insubordination to do what was culturally and professionally right, in an environment where so much was systemically wrong. There were teachers who would communicate to white thought leaders and philanthropists a commitment to an intellectually limiting model of education, but would still subversively include topics like Latin and Greek in their curricula.[19]

As a teacher and school leader, I had no idea that Hampton University and other colleges and universities also took in Indigenous students. Many Native Americans found that in order to succeed in these non-Native school environments, they would be stripped of their identity, land, and language. However, HBCUs were just a cog in the wheel of a Native American assimilationist doctrine, led by prominent white leaders and policy makers. More widely, a network of Indian boarding schools across the country, including primary, secondary, and post-secondary schools, were a physical and psychological assault on Native American ways of being, teaching, and learning.[20]

As early model HBCUs like Hampton were starting to rise, the commitment to Reconstruction started to weaken. In 1883, the U.S. Supreme Court, through a series of five court cases, commonly referred to as The Civil Rights Cases, unraveled the work done by the Thirteenth and Fourteenth Amendments barring slavery and servitude, and declared that all citizens are afforded equal protections under state and federal laws. How were the rights of Black and brown people undermined through these cases? The Court ruled that the Amendments did not bar private citizens from practicing racial discrimination, officially ushering in the era of Jim Crow and bringing an end to the time of Reconstruction. When Reconstruction officially became a discontinued commitment, white segregationist politicians didn't shut down the Black schools, but they did make sure they were underfunded and permanently separate, setting the stage for Jim Crow,[21] and in turn calcifying the patterns and experiences Black educators and students still encounter today.

Brown v. Board of Education, Topeka, Kansas

When I think about the history of education for Black and brown children in America, I often reflect on the fact that The Civil Rights Cases in 1883 set the stage for the century and a half of education to follow. From 1952 to 1954, in efforts led by the NAACP, several families came together to challenge the separate but equal laws established by the 1890 *Plessy v. Ferguson* ruling. Until the U.S. Supreme Court ruled on the *Brown v. Board of Education* cases, Black families across the country, but mainly in the South, were forced to attend underfunded schools while their tax dollars went to support white schools they were legally unable to attend. Furthermore, Latinx, Asian American, and Indigenous families across the country also faced systemic discrimination and saw the courts as their only recourse for obtaining the kind of education their children deserved.

In 1927, the U.S. Supreme Court ruled in the case of *Lum v. Rice*, upholding the discrimination of *Plessy v. Ferguson* and classifying the Lum family, who were Chinese, as colored. The Lums lived in Mississippi and only had two options for their daughter's education: white-only schools or colored schools. Understanding that self-identifying with Black people would solidify their place as second-class citizens, the Lums chose a white school, Rosedale School in Bolivar County, which would ultimately kick their daughter out. *Lum v. Rice* was the first of the education desegregation cases to reach the Supreme Court.[22]

Twenty years after the *Lum v. Rice* ruling, the Mendez family of California found themselves facing yet another instance of educational discrimination. Though this Mexican and Puerto Rican family was technically categorized as white, their child was pushed out of the school and told that she would have to attend a separate school for Mexican children. The resulting court case, *Mendez v. Westminster,* was yet another significant U.S. Supreme Court ruling that laid down the precedent for *Brown v. Board of Education.*

The Mendez family successfully sought protection under the
Fourteenth Amendment based on language discrimination. Both *Lum
v. Rice* and *Mendez v. Westminster* were cases fraught with an
interwoven web of anti-Black, anti-Indigenous, and anti-Asian
undertones that underscored both the commonalities and frictions
that existed between and within racial and ethnic groups in our
country due to America's color caste system. Sometimes, it is hard to
imagine that court rulings from over sixty years ago could still impact
our classrooms today, but the resulting policies and laws deeply
influence the realities of our Black and brown students.

Across the country and throughout these two rulings, Black
children were forced to learn from outdated curricular materials
because their districts would not invest in their education and instead
provided hand-me-down books that often had pages missing and
vulgar messages written on their pages. This problem of limited access
to high-quality educational materials has not changed much in
recent years.

We celebrate *Brown v. Board of Education, Topeka, Kansas,* as a
groundbreaking case, and we should. *Brown* is perhaps one of the
most significant court cases since the Emancipation Proclamation.
And while *Brown* opened the door to dismantle Jim Crow in
education, it provided the promise for progress while simultaneously
endangering the psyche of Black children across the nation. In fact,
the often underexplored *Brown v. Board II* decision was a result of
local and state level backlash against the call for mandatory
integration, leading to more leniency about intentionally integrating,
creating more space for creative discrimination and educational
malpractice.[23]

As W.E.B. Du Bois opined in "Does the Negro Need Separate
Schools?" (1935), Black children would be forced to be educated by
those who do not believe they are capable of learning. In addition to
Du Bois, Anna Julia Cooper, Zora Neale Hurston, and Carter G.

Woodson also had reservations and nuanced thoughts about integration. *Brown* was the first time Black children came face to face with people whose job it was to educate them; however, the majority of these educators had no faith in Black children's ability to learn. Perhaps even more insidious—in my own school experience, as well as Mitchell's—was that those white educators believed that Black children did not bring cultural lenses or experiences. Instead, these educators insisted on the absence of both. I experienced this both as a Black student growing up in a predominantly white Midwestern community, where I was rewarded for every assimilationist and disciplined behavior, and embarrassed by ways of engaging that were particular to my culture and made to believe that any aspect of my culture was forbidden in the school and classroom space. That was surely the case upon the inception of the *Brown v. Board*, and one could argue it continues to this day. Such an ideology shaped the instructional practices used for centuries.

Is it any wonder we are facing a reckoning about cultural relevance right now, in classrooms like Mitchell's or the ones I observed in Louisiana? Is it at all confusing why it is so difficult for many teachers, especially white teachers, to fully understand the need for attending to the identity of the children who sit in front of them? Is it any wonder we stand on the precipice of dismantling a structure designed for inequity? Simply put and as I mentioned earlier, it was built on a caste system using racist ideology as its delivery mechanism, relying on faulty science that equated skull size to intellectual capacity.[24]

Not only did *Brown* offer promises and problems for students of color, particularly Black children, but also for Black teachers, who championed Black intellectual development but bore the brunt of the effects of desegregation. As a result of the *Brown* decision, nearly 40,000 African-American teachers and school leaders lost their jobs between 1954 and 1963, which accounted for nearly one-third of the

Black teaching force.[25] This loss reverberated deeply for Black children and families, because with the reduction in Black educators came the erosion of compassionate, rigorous, and community-based instruction.

This seismic reduction in the Black teaching force after 1954 was no accident. School desegregation meant Black teachers could potentially teach white students, and communities were not going to allow that shift to happen, because the only socially acceptable place for Black adults to have control of white children was in the realm of domestic caretaking. This had a cascading effect on the infrastructure of Black teachers' unions and networks, which, along with the connections and best practices they maintained, either collapsed or were folded into traditionally white teachers' unions and networks.

The rule, via Jim Crow and similar policy measures, was that Black teachers could not teach white students, and less qualified white teachers were fine to teach Black students. Despite Black teachers on average being more highly educated than their white counterparts, Jim Crow laws rendered them vulnerable. There was also an unspoken but widely applied rule that if the Black teacher was well qualified, they would not be allowed to teach; thus many qualified Black teachers found themselves unemployed. Additionally, Black principals could not lead predominantly white schools.

Once again, our national past has laid the ground for our present educational reality. Today roughly only 7%[26] of all public school teachers are Black, yet Black students make up roughly 15%[27] of all public school students—a disparity that was legislated and designed. Now, when considering *Brown v. Board* and the Black teaching force, I often think of Audre Lourde, when she stated, "the master's tools will never dismantle the master's house."[28] Lourde challenged us to understand that the "master" might allow some progress; however, genuine progress would require using a different set of tools.

Using the master's tools would result in the appearance of progress while leading us to the place the master had designed all along.

To ensure effective teaching for Black and brown students, we must teach every child through the lens of their full humanity. Unfortunately, the legacies and structures left behind from centuries of our country's racial caste system continue to make this idea almost revolutionary.

Nothing New Under the Sun

What have now become common practices—collaboration, child centeredness, the need for adherence to the emotional development of the child, and learning as a tool for meaning-making about the world—are central to many other cultures, but not in the Western European, production-centered structures that shape the American education system.[29] When these more holistic educational practices are "rediscovered" in our modern education system, they are talked about as if they're new, instead of acknowledged for their roots in other cultures. African, Indigenous, and others throughout time have relied heavily on these constructs to teach their own communities.

One of the reasons it may have been hard for me, early on in my career, to name what I had experienced and saw in classrooms I observed, is that we are led to believe that all we know about education flows from the minds and mouths of European-descended researchers and educational philosophers. All cultures bring a set of learning structures that they believe reflect their values and ensure its continuation. While non-white culture in many American schools is reserved for special days of the year, the cultural norms of different racial and ethnic groups shapes students' daily lives and become the driving factors of how they understand themselves. What does this mean for us today, as educators who are ready to reflect not only on the history but on the larger, European-normed culture in which we still live today?

What does it mean to want to knock down those foundations and replace them with stronger, sturdier materials for the children we teach?

As I've learned more and more about how the historical legacies of education have impacted my own educational experience, first as a student and later as a teacher, I am now acutely aware of the messages that taught me to doubt my own cultural ways of knowing and learning. Maybe even more importantly, when I became an educator, those messages, compounded throughout my life, deeply impacted the layers I brought to my classroom—even as a Black woman.

3 Learning at the Intersections: Race and Standards

What do my experiences at Mitchell's school, our learning about the foundations of history, and our exploring of systems of power influencing our earliest experiences mean for teachers in the classroom today?

As a little girl, I would hear my elders say, "There is nothing new under the sun." Everything we think is new or just discovered has been here, in some form, before. What we have picked up, marveled at, and been introduced to, has in fact just evolved from what already was. This rings particularly true when I think about the experience of watching Mitchell wither in his classroom. That feeling of shame and exclusion, the message of "You don't count here," was a replica of my school experience and what research has shown many students of color experience in schools.

Even my conversation with Mitchell's teacher and her professed color-blindness were nothing new; both her colorblind lens and her belief that Black people didn't have a culture was an outgrowth of the racial caste system that undergirds the formation of this country, a caste system that, even in its earliest stages, mimicked the artificial intelligence that we rely on today. Systemic racism evolves as it observes and predicts our intentions, and then transforms those beliefs into actions that reinforce caste. Just like AI, the caste system regenerates itself, by processing data and filtering it through the biased norms we, as a society, feed it. The system of racism that determines how we operate schools and who gets the optimal experience from those schools, is constantly evolving to maintain itself. Systemic racism reforms and morphs with every passing day, year, and decade; it informs us and we inform it.

I don't believe Mitchell's teacher woke up on the morning of my observation with the intention of inflicting psychological trauma on Mitchell; quite the opposite, she believed she was creating a classroom structured for student success. However, how she designed that model of success was informed by her deeply rooted implicit beliefs about Black children. Without checking how she arrived at those beliefs, the immediacy and unconsciousness of her actions drove responses that would have far-reaching consequences for Mitchell and the classmates who look like him. She was not a bad person, or even a bad teacher; however, her choices in that classroom supported a system of racial harm. If we are ever to dismantle the predictability of achievement by race, it is vital for us to stop and examine the systems in which we work and live.

Fighting Against the Norm

Very early in my career, I had the extraordinary opportunity to engage with a school that held some of the highest expectations of learning that I have ever seen. I graduated from Florida A&M University, a public, Historically Black University (HBCU), whose teacher residency program at the time encouraged us to look outside of our local school systems and "traditional" teaching residencies and to instead seek schools that would support us in expanding our perceptions of what it meant to be an educator. For instance, if you wanted to teach in your hometown, you might be encouraged to take a residency abroad; if you were moving to an urban context, you might be prompted to try a rural residency and vice versa. I was accepted into a residency program in Cincinnati, Ohio, at the prestigious Marva Collins Preparatory School.

My professor and friends pushed me to do my residency at Marva Collins Preparatory School because I was interested in serving students in large urban settings. They wanted me to start in a setting where the possibilities were endless for Black and brown students. Marva Collins was an educator and mother who became fed up with the Chicago Public Schools system in which her children were enrolled. She turned her frustration and educational experience into the fuel needed to create Westside Preparatory School, which she founded in 1975 at a local college and then moved to her own home.[1] In a 1981 interview Collins explained, "I felt that there were far too many children being recruited for failure, far too many excuses for not educating."[2]

Although the Cincinnati campus was not the original preparatory school that Marva Collins started, it still upheld the tenets of her pedagogical practices, the rigor of classroom content, and high expectations for its students. On the first day, the founder of the Cincinnati sister campus, Mrs. Mims, started by giving me a tour of the school. There was one teacher per grade at this K–5 grade school, and each teacher matriculated with their students as they progressed to the next grade. The first teacher we encountered was teaching kindergarten because the first class of students she'd ushered through had just moved on to sixth grade.

I started my residency there in January and, already, the kindergarteners I observed on the first day were reading books that were at least at a first-grade, if not second-grade, level. In fact, they were flying through them. Marva Collins's methodology stood squarely on the components of what we now know as the "science of reading." According to The Reading League, "the science of reading is a vast, interdisciplinary body of scientifically-based research about reading and issues related to [teaching] reading and writing."[3] I witnessed teachers at the Marva Collins Preparatory school utilizing the five elements essential to effectively teaching reading: phonological awareness, phonics, fluency, vocabulary, and reading comprehension. Unlike the 3Qing approach to reading pedagogy that began in the 1960s, the science of reading is grounded in neurological science. It amplifies how our human brains acquire spoken and written language and "is culminated in a preponderance of evidence to inform how proficient reading and writing develop; why some have difficulty; and how we can most effectively assess and teach and, therefore, improve student outcomes through prevention of and intervention for reading difficulties."[4] Though the Marva Collins schools did not label their work with this title, they nonetheless were grounded in these proven approaches.

This Marva Collins class was set up like a regular kindergarten classroom, with one major difference: in addition to posters of letters and colors hanging on the walls, there were full words, covers of books, and writing from the students themselves adorning the room. It was obvious those principles of reading were at work in every classroom.

In the combined second- and third-grade classrooms, where I was later assigned, the reading level was so advanced, and the teacher so skillful in adjusting the cognitive load for students, I couldn't tell who was a second grader and who was a third grader. My residency experience indoctrinated me into the belief that to build the foundations of reading fluency for all students, it is essential that instruction be based on the science of reading. This belief would become a central part of our work at UnboundEd, where we lean on the call to action of Dr. L. C. Moats. Moats proposes that as students become better readers, they in turn become better writers, which pushes their reading even further. Without the pertinent foundation of reading structures, students will not get miles on the page. We understand that to even start students on the path to becoming better readers, they must be given the foundational components of the science of reading.

On my first day of residency, in the second- and third-grade combined classroom, I observed the students tackling George Orwell's *Animal Farm*. In all lessons I saw at Marva Collins Preparatory School, students' culture, their neighborhoods, and their lived experiences were incorporated to help them understand what they were learning. In the case of *Animal Farm*, my lead teacher referenced the park near the school that was being shut down by a major corporation to acquire the land. What was happening locally—the political and local context—was all brought into that lesson, so that even in moments when these second- and third-grade students couldn't decode the vocabulary, they could understand the content and ideas around power and the fight for power. This expansive view of students' community and cultural knowledge, and the limitlessness of student potential, is perhaps the exact opposite of Mitchell's teacher's approach, including her refusal to allow Mitchell's cultural context to come into play in her classroom.

When I took over the second- and third-grade class for my part of the residency, we were starting a Shakespearean unit, and I was tasked with teaching *A Midsummer Night's Dream*. My panic started kicking in immediately: along with the original play, I must have read five different children's versions of the play, alongside the CliffNotes. I was so worried about not being ready to teach the students and about displaying my own mastery of the content that my guiding teacher had to pull me aside.

She told me, "You can't be afraid to learn alongside your students. You don't have to come in with all of the answers." She went on to remind me that the standards we were introducing the students to were focused on the structure of plays and character development in a story, and grounded in a commitment to giving the experience of Shakespeare. Therefore, it was even more important to allow my students to bring their lived experiences into the lesson, so that we could make connections as we learned together. Her reminder was not intended to diminish the importance of me understanding Shakespeare's writings, but to focus my attention on the standards of learning the students needed to be exposed to, to charge myself with learning the pedagogical content knowledge needed to facilitate that learning, and to use my students' cultural, linguistic, historical, and local context to support their understanding of learning. I was lucky to have her expertise by my side; as a practitioner, she wanted to ensure I would always be willing to expand my body of knowledge and my pedagogical approach. Just as students' learning was a never-ending cycle, my learning as an educator was also ongoing: the more exposure I got to content and specified standards, the better I would become at facilitating learning.

Of course, Marva Collins Preparatory was not perfect. Because of limited funding, the class sizes ranged somewhere between 36 to 40 students per teacher. However, the students knew the school had high expectations, and they were adequately prepared. And while these were not ideal classroom conditions, the drawbacks did not deter the school community from learning. True collective learning—where students played active roles in both teaching and learning—occurred in all of those classrooms. My residency began almost 20 years after Marva Collins opened her first school, but I learned that students and families chose Marva Collins Preparatory for many of the same reasons that led Marva Collins to found the school in the first place: they wanted to combat the lack of academic rigor, social support, and care in their other school sites. I also noticed that the educators at

Marva Collins Preparatory enrolled their own children in the school. Clearly, there was a deep investment, not only in the model, but in the vision set forth by school leaders like Mrs. Mims.

As a novice teacher, witnessing the learning and teaching at Marva Collins Preparatory was a transformative experience. On the first day, and every day after, that environment challenged me to ask myself what it took for me as an educator to uphold those high standards and demonstrate such love for my students. The productive struggle in those classrooms supported a level of intellect and engagement that challenged my own expectations for students who looked like me. Before that moment, I had thought I held high expectations for Black and brown children, but the Marva Collins methodology and, more importantly, the teachers' expectations for themselves as practitioners and for their students pushed me beyond what I thought was possible. Before my residency, when I imagined my career in teaching, I only ever imagined myself as a role model for Black children in the classroom. Marva Collins Preparatory helped me see myself as a practitioner of teaching.

Marva Collins Preparatory was incredible because Marva Collins thwarted both institutional and structural racism through adaptive and technical means. According to scholar Ronald Heifetz, "Technical problems, while often challenging, can be solved applying existing know-how and the organization's current problem-solving processes. Adaptive problems resist these kinds of solutions because they require individuals throughout the organization to alter their ways. . . ."[5] Marva Collins, and the teachers and leaders she trained, spoke often about students being the big "You" and teachers being the little "i," an adaptive philosophy focused on shifting power dynamics and mindsets in classrooms. Her schools focused on the idea of students as experts in their own thinking. This, alongside the daily mantras she used, reminded students, in particular Black and brown students, of their innate intelligence and abilities. Marva Collins quite literally spoke that shift into existence. Technically, her pedagogical choice to lean into literacy skills and phonetics was equally transformative. Her work proved to Chicago Public Schools and the country that the students they dismissed could not only get up to par, but thrive. At the core of her mission was her determination to build a school that countered every norm of institutional and structural racism.

Marva Collins's own professional evolution was history in action. Everything I've read since about the battles Black educators fought throughout American history to educate Black children was made manifest in her schools. As a child, I had experienced an integrated public school system in Dayton, Ohio. Collins's schools were the antithesis of that experience in almost every way. She and her educational contemporaries like Jaime Escalante in East Los Angeles proved to a doubtful nation that with high expectations, care, and a thorough understanding of their craft, they could help students—the same students the system had discarded—to excel.

And yet, even when armed with my incredible experience at Marva Collins Preparatory, even with an HBCU undergraduate education in which I was introduced to historical figures who shifted education in communities of color, even with the influence of many other researchers' work on culturally affirming pedagogy, I still found myself stifled when I formally entered the teaching force. Months after my teaching residency, I began teaching full-time at an elementary school in Marietta, Georgia. In my inaugural classroom of first graders, I was excited to use some of Marva Collins Preparatory's reading framework, specifically the systematic phonics program. Even though I didn't have all of the necessary materials, I used the attributes of the reading program that supported building the students' skills in phonological awareness while utilizing their cultural and linguistic backgrounds—and techniques like the choral reading Mitchell was so earnestly using—to ground the learning. In addition to incorporating activities that used the five elements essential to teaching reading, I utilized the sound cards and an alphabet rap that students practiced every morning as a warm up to our day. As a result, something amazing happened: my students' reading scores started shooting off the charts. Almost immediately, my success was met with pushback.

As excited as I was about implementing my newly learned resources and techniques, I was surprised to find myself at odds with the culture of my new school. The lead teacher in my grade level began reporting me for not following the laid out reading plans she had created for the teaching team. My school leader and supervisor, a Black woman as well, believed I was too ambitious. I was scolded for not following the adjusted lesson plans that the lead teacher had prepared.

"I don't know why you don't just use the lesson plans she's written out," she said.

When I was invited back the next year to teach my students as they moved up to second grade, my friend—a Black woman and the only other person of color on our six-person teaching team—told our colleagues, "We need to learn Lacey's reading program." She and I were met with passive aggressive silence and then peppered with questions clearly intended to shut the idea down. I could not understand why there would be such resistance to a framework of teaching that capitalized on researched and proven methods, maximized student engagement, and affirmed who our students were and could become. So I went home and typed out the whole reading program. When I brought it to school the next day, my principal threatened to fire me if I did not comply with the lesson plans that were already created by the grade-level lead teacher. It didn't matter that our students—many of whose families were experiencing extreme poverty or battling homelessness—were actually learning in my class. It mattered more that I comply.

At the time, our district actually didn't have a reading program. None of the teachers in my school, the lead teacher and myself included, were certified in reading. Because there was no systematic program in place, I knew it would help our students to use the tried-and-true Marva Collins approach. I see now that those teachers might have worried that they didn't have the skill to attempt a new reading curriculum. The prospect of learning this new skill must have felt uncomfortable. Then, all I knew was that I was being forced to comply with a system that did not work. In the same way that my students were forced to accept an education that did not prioritize their personhood, I, as a Black educator, was forced to comply with an educational strategy that did not work simply because it upheld the norms and practices of that institution and the broader system in which I worked.

I later learned in my career, while working in school systems serving families of higher socioeconomic status, that those teachers had far more professional learning experiences, materials, and support. But even with those additional resources, they also were not given the appropriate learning and training on not just the what, but also the *how* of teaching reading.

I now recognize that the missing link in my own teacher preparation and early teaching experiences was a grounding in the research—both about the neurological science and pedagogical practices that shape effective teaching. Without understanding that most of our brains acquire language in the same way, I didn't truly understand *how* students could effectively grow their reading fluency skills. Instead, I, like so many other educators, was using methodology that was popular, but not well researched. For instance, at the time I met Mitchell's teacher, I thought that Readers and Writers Workshop was the best way to get books in children's hands and help them amass "miles on the page." I bought into the idea (along with hundreds of thousands of educators), even though the

Readers and Writers Workshops weren't backed by research. In my mind, it was at least a way to ensure that Black and brown students had greater access to book rooms and libraries; however, we weren't *actually* teaching them how to read using scientific, research-based strategies. Without sound research, programs like Readers and Writers Workshop are like bringing someone to a pool or a beach—excited that we've given them an opportunity to be in the water—but not teaching them how to swim. As a sector, then and now, we do our students a disservice by not equipping our educators with the research and methodological foundation to best serve them.

Still, some teachers in more affluent schools were allowed to augment their reading pedagogy. But because our students were perceived as coming in at a disadvantage, there was less flexibility in how we could teach them. As we continue this work of equity, it is important for us to inquire: What drives leaders in systems to uphold policies, practices, and procedures that do not—and have not—produced the desired outcomes, especially when supporting students who have experienced the most disenfranchisement?

I learned a hard lesson that year: decisions made around students' learning were not predicated on the needs of the students, but rather on the comfort level of the adults. Too many of the adults I encountered that first year saw themselves as missionaries—coming into Black and brown communities to serve them—only to unwittingly become the foot of oppression on the backs of their students. What would it take for us to shift our society's view of teachers' professional position from missionaries to practitioners?

The Unwritten Rules

In many ways, the American teaching profession is set up with a trap door from the moment you enter it. In much of our national rhetoric, teachers are ethereal, self-sacrificing beings who don't have enough money or resources to do their jobs, but must make it work anyway. Many teachers are attracted to the profession because of this ideal of sacrifice. Others enter the profession moved to make a difference in the lives of students despite this perception of sacrifice. However, we are professionals, just like everyone else. As a country, our citizens don't expect, or even want, electricians or doctors to make do with so little. There are few other industries or professions that are built around the mechanism of sacrificing in the way that modern teaching is. As a result, we reward teachers who come into teaching to "save" their students, and we prioritize that sacrifice, instead of honoring their professionalism by teaching them how to be incredibly skilled practitioners.

Layered on top of this are the many implicit and explicit messages we receive about people of color in our society. If a teacher is sent into a school to save children, it is implied that there must be something wrong with them and their communities. This is the muck and mire that stains our schools and limits the ability for Black and brown children and children living in poverty to access affirming and rigorous instruction in their schools. Marva Collins Preparatory was the first place where I viewed myself outside of this model of endless sacrifice, and when I brought my new practitioner's lens to the school in Marietta, it was challenging for my colleagues. Acknowledging that they could expect brilliance from their students required that my fellow teachers shed their saviorism. I didn't understand it then, but now I understand that asking them to address their negative assumptions also brought up a lot of shame. It was easier to maintain the status quo, to proceed with lesson plans that were producing middling results, and to leave unexamined their standards for teacher and student performance.

When a school is set up so that expectations of students are subjugated to teacher performance or ideals of "classroom management," it becomes urgent for teachers to prove they are worthy of being in the building. Especially as a Black, brown, or otherwise marginalized teacher, entering into an environment in which you are one of few teachers of color brings automatic assumptions about who you are. Some colleagues assume you can and should "handle" the students of color or that you would be the educator best suited to "meet their needs." However, ideas about meeting student needs are very narrow: focusing on behavior and remediation, not exploration and acceleration. Over the years, I encountered white teachers in my building who expected me to be the disciplinarian ("Can you come talk to Tyrik for me?") or the translator for Black and brown students. As a young Black teacher, I felt if I didn't meet this expectation, I might be failing my students and in danger of losing my job. If we are ever to truly transform our teaching community into a body that is more reflective of the racially, ethnically, and linguistically diverse society we live in, then we need to ensure that our work not only acknowledges the commodity of familiar backgrounds these teachers have with their students, but also supports them as professionals in their evolution as educators.

For many teachers of color, the threat and urgency of being a representative begins to overtake you and can obscure the opportunities to deliver transformational instruction. Institutional racism works to silence and to scold, even as structural racism determines the policies, practices, and procedures governing student learning. Remember the analogy we used of structural racism as the orchestra? Here, in plain terms, structural racism shaped a musical score that meant certain failure for Black and brown children. Meanwhile, the institutional racism at play in my school building maintained its part of the melody, no matter the cost to children or teachers. Systemic racism affects the lives, well-being, and life chances of people of color. It normalizes historical, cultural, and institutional practices that benefit white people and disadvantage people of color. As a young teacher, I didn't have the language to say what I know

now: Marva Collins Preparatory School refused to be structured around institutional racism, whereas my first paid teaching experience was built completely around the lenses and structures of institutional racism.

Every morning during my residency at Marva Collins Preparatory School, our students recited a mantra, one that students at every Marva Collins Preparatory school were expected to memorize. Some thirty years later, there are valid critiques about some of its messages around personal choice, but the first morning I heard it, I cried. I had never heard anything like it said aloud by Black children in a school setting. To this day I can still recite it. Here are a few lines from the creed:

> Society will draw a circle that shuts me out, but my superior thoughts will draw me in. I was born to win if I do not spend too much time trying to fail. I will ignore the tags and names given to me by society since only I know what I have the ability to become.
>
> My success and my education can be companions that no misfortune can depress, no crime can destroy, and no enemy can alienate. Without education, man is a slave, a savage wandering from here to there believing whatever he is told.
>
> Time and chance come to us all. I can be either hesitant or courageous. I can swiftly stand up and shout: "This is my time and my place. I will accept the challenge."[6]

But when I tried to emulate Marva Collins's work, I got eaten up by the system. It was not enough for me to be a beacon of light. For the students in my grade level and school to thrive, the system needed to recognize the need for justice that is found in the details of its teaching and learning.

Justice in the Details

To seek, identify, and create schools where *justice is found in the details of teaching and learning*®, it is necessary that we stand on a common definition of equity. Here at UnboundEd, we understand that equity, simply stated, is the assurance that everyone is receiving a fair shot in an existing system. Unfortunately, none of us have seen a completely equitable education system yet, on any measure, be it race, gender, disability status, class, or any of the numerous junctures of any of these. However, the lack of a perfect model does not mean we should abandon the constant pursuit of justice, both in our own classrooms and in the education system more broadly. There are schools today whose work closely emulates the equitable education experiences I witnessed at the Marva Collins Preparatory School, and it is necessary that we seek them out to help us reimagine what aspects of justice in education can look like.

Mrs. Mims and her colleagues in Cincinnati understood that the way to an equitable education is not just through the "best" pedagogical practices, and it cannot be delivered with high-quality materials and curriculum alone. Their work illustrates that siloed and disconnected diversity, equity, and inclusion efforts are not enough to radically shift classroom and school system practices. Instead, equitable education must be built through intentional practice. There must be explicit communication and shared commitment to the kind of inclusiveness that is needed when we say equity.

At UnboundEd, we believe *justice is found in the details of teaching and learning*®. There are many roads to social justice, and ours begins at the intersection of high-quality curriculum, standards, and content that gives a full perspective of the global majority, pedagogical practices, and the equity needed to eliminate the predictability of educational outcomes by race. At UnboundEd, we envision a world in which educators actively work together to dismantle systemic racism by providing grade-level, engaging, affirming, and meaningful instruction. We focus on the students who have historically been pushed to the margins, in order for all students to benefit and thrive. We do this to ensure we can enact a more just educational system that not only allows students to bring their whole selves to learning, but opens up opportunities to engage and learn about cultures outside their own. It is necessary that all students be prepared to move into a multiethnic, multilinguistic, global, college and career trajectory outside of their own.

"Justice is found in the details of teaching and learning®" is our rallying cry, at UnboundEd. It is where we begin to understand the "discretionary spaces," as coined by Dr. Deborah Ball,[7] in which we teach students. It is the moment-to-moment decisions we make when students are sitting before us. In those moments, we can interrogate the beliefs we hold as educators about our students and ourselves as practitioners, so that we do not turn those beliefs into actions that further the disenfranchisement of those same students.

For instance, if there are lessons where we remove the cognitive dissonance of critical thinking questions and replace those questions with those requiring a simple "yes" or "no" answer, we should be curious about why we are doing so. Is it motivated by our beliefs? Are we lifting the cognitive load to get to the goal of the lesson? Being curious about our underlying beliefs may reveal that we are expecting less of our students, thus perpetuating injustices that will compound throughout their education. Through my work at UnboundEd, I have come to believe that when we come together as a community, adhering to charges that center our development as educators, we can then begin to dismantle the policies, practices, and procedures that systematize implicit bias and biased/racist overtones. While this implicit bias is often activated in our teaching and learning, if we choose to examine it, we are not powerless against it. When we act together, we embrace our power and push against the systemic racism that shapes all of our lives.

We must be equipped with the ability to examine our materials, practices, and beliefs to ensure we are not regenerating learning environments that create the predictability of achievement by race. In my conversations with Mitchell's teacher, she was reaching out for help, acknowledging that there were vital instruments missing from her knapsack of teacher practice. It took many years as a teacher, school leader, and system-wide professional development specialist for me to finally understand that the instructional core of teaching *had* to be intertwined with equity. And that combined approach, when braided with pedagogical mindsets and tools, evolved into my work with districts on a larger scale as CEO of UnboundEd. Working collaboratively with colleagues who have a shared vision of shrinking inequity in schools across the country, we created five charges—five practical action steps every educator can take—to support teachers like Mitchell's, my colleagues in Marietta, and, quite frankly, my younger teaching self. These charges raise our consciousness levels so that we, as educators, do not succumb to the bias and stereotypes embedded in the systems surrounding our students and ourselves. If justice is found in the details, our plans must focus on those details if we are to be successful in dismantling the predictability of achievement by race in our schools.

The Five Charges

My experience at Marva Collins Preparatory gave me a better understanding of the mechanics of what I should teach my students and how I could structure that experience to be identity-affirming. My experiences in Marietta—and in countless other schools since— have demonstrated how hard it is to put that ideal into practice. Mitchell's teacher wanted to make a radical shift in her classroom, but she simply didn't know how to, and there were rules, structures, ideas, and attitudes within the system that disincentivized her from trying. In addition to the work of transforming her mindset, she admitted to me that she also lacked pedagogical training.

She asked me simply, "Can you help me?" And I did work with her to try to make a drastically different classroom experience for Mitchell and his classmates. But if I were to meet her for the first time today, I would have a more concrete answer for her. Back then, I still had to learn many of the frameworks that would be necessary to support her. And it would not be until I led an education organization, UnboundEd, that my team and I could even begin to create and use those frameworks.

For many years, as we trained teachers about culturally relevant curricula and combating bias in the classroom, I received pushback from both teachers and administrators. Their most frequent request was "Can you just tell us how to get our students out of their achievement gaps?" Questions like this one distract us, as educators, from the systemic norms that created the gaps we are witnessing. Maybe even more importantly, this kind of framing around achievement gaps prevents us from interrogating our own personal relationship with those same systems. As I've deeply explored my own biases, privileges, and wounds at the hands of our education system, this understanding has led me to reorient my approach both as an educator and a coach of other educators.

As Dr. Gloria Ladson-Billings says, "The first problem teachers confront is believing that successful teaching of poor students of color is primarily about 'what to do.' Instead, I suggest that the problem is rooted in how we think—about the social context, about the students, about the curriculum, and about instruction."[8] Dr. Ladson-Billings pushes us to reconsider what to do with curricula because, as she urges us to remember, curriculum is culture. Curriculum, like the rest of our educational structures, is an artifact of many historical legacies and holds the lenses of its designers and authors. Therefore, we must examine: What does our curriculum communicate to our students? How can we design pedagogy that ignites an organic love of learning in all children? What is happening in our pedagogical practices that reinforces rather than dismantles biases? How can we address unfinished instruction in the context of grade-level learning?

UnboundEd's journey to equity in education started with the adoption of the Common Core Standards beginning around 2009. We believed then, and still do, that one facet of ensuring that all students receive an equitable education was through the enactment of the standards. Early on in our organizational development, we realized that standards-aligned instruction would be impossible without first starting with an aligned curriculum. With the help of other organizations and notable curriculum developers, a group of former educators developed the EngageNY curriculum. We landed on the premise that starting with an aligned curriculum would provide educators the baseline for attending to the language of the standards. Working with New York State, our goal was to support districts and educators in math and ELA instruction of the Common Core standards. Educators could dedicate more time to adapting an aligned curriculum instead of creating one from scratch. As others began to adopt the EngageNY curriculum in states across the nation, we continued to believe, and see in practice, that this was the path to closing the opportunity gap.

We also continued to examine the realities for students of color in our nation's public schools. In 2016, UnboundEd began a review of TNTP's research on students' access to grade-level instruction. After sifting through The New Teacher Project (TNTP) and the National Assessment of Educational Progress (NAEP) data, we saw that the research underscored what we had already observed in the field: that students of color did not have adequate access to grade-level curriculum, tasks that would propel their academic identities adequately, or lessons that would prepare them for the demands of college and career.

We saw that when districts and schools rolled out aligned curricula, they often enacted the curriculum by gutting it of grade-level tasks and rigor. Many educators lowered the rigor within mathematical tasks or modified the grade-level reading within standards-aligned curriculum as an attempt to address unfinished instruction. Looking at this adaptive challenge from a global perspective, we realized that educator beliefs impact instructional outcomes for students. We realized that implicit bias was at the root of deficit ideologies about the capabilities of students and educators of color, and this bias fueled structural racism in education. The question then was not "What is wrong with these teachers?" but "What should we consider in terms of their professional development?" We would not learn to replace that first, bias-fueled question until we supported schools and educators to systematically identify and examine bias.

To address implicit bias within education systems, we first had to address it within our own organization. We had to hold a mirror up to our own mindsets, practices, and strategies that perpetuated structural racism. As we did so, we slowly began to chip away at the adaptive challenge of undoing racism within the nonprofit world. We educated ourselves about racism externally and internally, which to this day includes intentional and continuous learning about anti-racism and its application to practice. This led to a complete revision of our public-facing messages to ensure pursuing equity and addressing systemic racism was at the center of the mission statement and development of the five charges. We began to ground all of our internal and external learning opportunities with an educational philosophy known as the intersection of the standards, content, aligned curriculum, and the equitable instructional practices essential for closing the opportunity gap caused by systemic bias and racism. Through the intersection we defined the "what," but we still needed to define the "how."

While we were off to an admirable start, it was not enough to support systematic change on a national playing field. In addition to our anti-racist work, we needed to include experts of color who dedicated their lives to making education not only accessible but relevant. Leaning on the tenets of Dr. Gloria Ladson-Billings, we honed in on the three pillars of Culturally Relevant Teaching: academic success, cultural competence, and socio-political consciousness.

We began to build our research based on culturally relevant teaching and recognized more current adaptations such as culturally responsive and sustaining pedagogy. By drawing connections between the key tenets of culturally relevant teaching, our educational philosophy, and years of anti-racist professional development, we landed on the "how." How could we express the mindset, practices, and strategies both educators and leaders would need to adopt in order to disrupt systemic racism and its impact on Black and brown students and educators of color? For this matter, we landed on GLEAM™, an approach to curriculum design and professional growth that can help educators and schools implement **g**rade-**l**evel, **e**ngaging, **a**ffirming, and **m**eaningful instruction—a practice where it is evident that *justice is found in the details of teaching and learning®*.

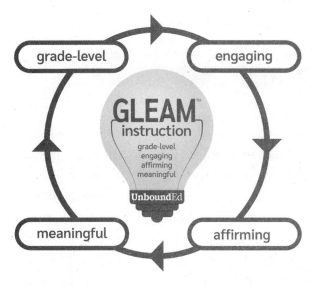

GLEAM™

Source: © UnboundEd Learning, Inc.

We believe this is just good teaching. And understanding what is at the heart of good teaching is what led us to GLEAM and the five charges for educator practice that act as its foundation. We take a deeper dive into the GLEAM framework in Chapter 5.

The two work together in more constructive ways to further justice in your classroom or school. Let's begin with the five charges. For example, when Mitchell's teacher admitted to me that day that she was lacking in pedagogical training and simply asked me, "Can you help me?," today I would start her professional development with the five charges.

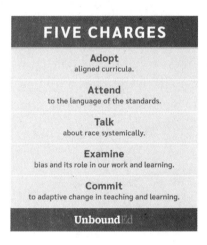

The first of the five charges is to **adopt aligned curricula**. The goal of this charge is to really focus us, as educators, on selecting instructional materials that correspond effectively with the skills students need to know. For those who do—or can become involved in—course adoption for your school or district, this can become a significant shift. For individual educators, Open Education Resources (OER)—like the Engage New York curriculum co-created with UnboundEd staff and partners—are free and open to the public and can be used to supplement existing curricula. Adoption implies building a relationship with the curriculum, finding its underpinnings and mechanics, so you as an educator can become an expert in how to execute it. Each grade unit and lesson is built upon the preceding grade-level skills and prepares students for the needed skills in the grade level to come. When adopting an aligned curriculum, it is vital to ensure that students' learning is mapped out within that staircase of complexity.

This is the very first charge because we no longer accept that—if your district does not have standards-aligned curriculum—your district's curriculum is the only one available to you. In this incredible age of technology, educators have greater access than ever to curricula that are innovative, high-quality, and grade-level appropriate. As an educator, all of the information you need to identify the level of rigor, or lack thereof, in your state, district, and school standards is available online. I include resources at the back of the book to support the search for High-Quality Instructional Materials (HQIM). Of course, my colleagues and I recognize that as individual teachers, you may not always have the power or authority to utilize HQIM in your classroom; however, it is still important for you to analyze, study, and review High-Quality Instructional Materials. Through that study and analysis, you will build your own awareness of the staircase of complexity necessary for students to navigate their educational careers successfully. Familiarizing yourself with HQIM builds your own pedagogical knapsack as an educator.

My colleagues and I also recognize that our current Open Education Resources, high-quality curriculum, and materials may be missing an essential aspect to seeking justice in the details. That is to say, much of our current curriculum and materials has been written through a white-dominant cultural lens. Even if there are multicultural authors, themes, illustrations, photographs, or historical content present, students and educators often experience them through a deficit viewpoint of a race or a lens that misrepresents ethnic groups' current and historical contributions to our society. It is essential for us to call this out, so that we may ask ourselves and others to analyze cultural blind spots found in our current materials. Just as importantly, there need to be specific and intentional steps to create curriculum and materials that justly and fairly represent our global society.

This first charge—adopting aligned curriculum—is a reminder that you are empowered and you don't have to rely solely on your school system's choices to grow your own pedagogical skill set. Open source and curricular tools like Open Education Resources exist so individuals and systems of educators can access a free curriculum that is standards-aligned. Open source curricula allow you to ask important questions such as: What are all of the components of this curriculum? Who wrote this curriculum? What standards is this curriculum pushing? One of the most powerful questions put forth by Dr. Gloria Ladson Billings is: What cultural artifacts does this curriculum include? From whose viewpoint or ideology is it told?[9] These are powerful tools, because even if your school system is using a curriculum that is not standards aligned, you can look at Open Education Resources materials to supplement your resources and make the decisions to give your students standards-aligned instruction.

I know that for many educators this is a scary and, quite frankly, tiring decision; it means you may have to swim upstream alone. Many of your schools and districts are married to the way things are, much like my school in Marietta was so many years ago. Those districts demand that you utilize curricula and materials that oftentimes are chosen out of political motivations or misinformed choices. Although my grade-level and school leaders thwarted my ideas of a reading program that adhered to the "code" of reading, they could not take away the knowledge I gained from studying at the Marva Collins Preparatory School. What I would have liked to use in a more formal reading program, I folded into my pedagogical moves, so as to ensure my students had the essential tools they needed to become lifelong readers. In this charge, we are not asking you to place yourselves in positions that could jeopardize your livelihood; we are passing along information that we know has shifted many of our colleagues' practices and beliefs. The first step is to try and use that information in a way that can move your own classroom and school forward toward an aligned and more equitable curriculum. Even if that starts with doing some research to find out how much flexibility you have in aligning your own practices, the more teachers who begin this work, the more likely it is that better adoption practices can grow in your school, district, and beyond.

The second charge is to **attend to the language of the standards**. This is powerful because it asks you as an educator to become armed with what the exact goal of each lesson is. What is it that your third grader needs to know to understand the third-grade standard you're covering? Where are they going, but, most importantly, where should they be coming from? What knowledge should they have gained prior to entering their current grade? Attending to the language of standards allows us to create a stair step of preparedness. Standards concept maps help you as an educator to look at the prerequisites that your students should have learned in their previous classrooms, and they help you deeply understand where they should be going before entering their next grade. Most importantly, when you turn this tool over to your students, so they are armed with the knowledge of what they are supposed to learn, the possibilities are endless. That's right, sharing with students "This is the standard you will learn in my class" gives them agency. In the language of Marva Collins, it turns them into the big "you" and you as a teacher into the little "i." I often think of how the Louisiana math classroom I visited might have been different had those students understood what they should be learning. Instead of a classroom of near catatonic students, how could engagement and agency have transformed that lesson?

I'd like to pause and define what a "standard" is, not because the idea is new to educators, but because the term is sometimes misconstrued and politicized in the news and we are going to keep this professional and straightforward. In the simplest terms, a standard is what a student is expected to know and be able to do at specific stages of their learning development. There is a lot of debate regarding whether standards can be ascribed to a specific teaching practice, curriculum, or assessment. As practitioners, we urge you to think of a standard in its simplest form, so that the justice found in the details can be examined and applied. We use standards every day: for instance, when we drive on the right side of the road or even when we place our items in our own cart while grocery shopping. While we have personal agency in how we dress, arrive at our destinations, and decide what we use to pack our grocery items, those individual decisions or personal opinions do not detract from our communal understanding of the standards. For instance, it would be confusing if I tried to put my broccoli in someone else's shopping cart. Standards communicate what students should know.

When you attend to the language of standards, as a teacher you have immediate knowledge about grade-level expectations and prerequisites, which better prepares you to recognize and address unfinished instruction. You can ask: Are there individuals in my classroom who have unfinished learning that prohibits them from achieving this standard? Who will require more support, and how can it be provided in the context of grade-level learning? As you plan your lessons, you make decisions about what scaffolding is necessary, how to break up larger concepts into chunks, and how to build knowledge based on what students already know. As educators, we should be careful about overprescribing remedial course work, if it is not required by a student's individual learning plan. Scaffolding in your lesson planning ensures that you are not moving off of the grade-level teaching standard into remedial coursework. Just-in-time scaffolding—the adjustments that happen in the classroom as needed—allows you to make decisions in front of your students, armed with the knowledge of what they do and don't have. We'll dive deeper into how to build scaffolding in our upcoming chapters on GLEAM™.

The third charge is to **talk about race systematically in your system**. This charge is about the implications and outcomes of the systematic bias and racism that are already at play in our school systems. In addition to a symphony, Dr. Beverly Tatum often describes racism and bias as smog. We all inhale the smog of racism and bias, and manifest it in implicit and explicit ways in our beliefs and actions. Structural and institutional racism are indeed real. There are existing frameworks and lenses that can help you as an educator, and your school system as a whole, to decode where institutional racism is impacting your students. Those frameworks and the definitions you use to combat institutional racism must be consistent to be effective. Anti-racist frameworks, for instance, can help you and your colleagues have effective and productive discussions about the construct of race.

Let's look at an example of how school culture itself can shift as a result of this intentional work. For decades as a nation, we've been consistent in advocating for girls in science, technology, engineering, and math (STEM). This discourse has become a critical part of how we structure opportunities in those subjects. And while there is still a long way to go, we've seen gains and a shift in how educators and administrators think about gender equity in math and science. We need to become just as fluent in our conversations about race as we've become about gender in STEM.

Over the past decade or so, the education sector has become well versed in talking about the impact of racial bias in school discipline, but it is not as practiced in addressing how those same systematic biases show up in instructional spaces. Some school districts' refusal to fully embrace racial equity frameworks and methodologies means we rarely talk about race systematically. This absence of dialogue is evident in our current national conversations about Critical Race Theory, which posits conversations about race as somehow antagonistic to learning. However, I would argue that equitable instruction is a part of the instructional core. In fact, it is the lack of these critical conversations throughout our education system's history that has eroded the instructional core. Self-examination is an essential part of teaching; for instance, without examination of our gender biases we would continue to accept the false assertion that, "girls just don't like math or science." How then do we tackle similarly false equivalencies like "Black kids are just not smart enough to get into AP"? Only with concerted and systemized discourse about race, bias, and historic disenfranchisement.

Without practiced racial frameworks, the education sector writ large doesn't have a means to push back against those who would seek to eradicate critical histories and curricula. Talking about race systematically means examining our own biases along with our colleagues', which leads us to courageous conversations about our beliefs and how they impact the decisions we make about the content, context, and pedagogy we craft for our students. This means setting up structures of dialogue with our colleagues, parents, board members, and communities that can make conversations like the one I had with Mitchell's teacher a normal occurrence. These conversations are meant to support each other as we move out of shame and fragility and into purpose and action.

The work of racial equity cannot simply be a one-and-done professional development session at the beginning of the year. Instead, these frameworks have to be consistently used to interrogate our educational institutions, to unearth inequity, and then to correct biased policies, practices, and procedures. There must also be specified moments to look at our nation's history, particularly how that history has either been ignored or extinguished. All of this plays a role in our beliefs, intentions, and actions. Our diversity, equity, and inclusion learning at UnboundEd always includes examining the legacies of racism and bias that exist in our policies, practices, and procedures. We are better positioned to critique the current systems we work and live in when we ask: Is this policy a technical solution to uphold de facto segregation in our district? How does our inaction support or perpetuate the Asian "model minority" myth? Is this school procedure necessary, or does it focus too heavily on dominant cultural norms? Are our language-acquisition frameworks sending messages to our multilingual students that they inherently have a deficit as an English language learner? We have to be vigilant and diligent about watching where aspects of systematically racist policies, practices, and procedures show up.

The fourth charge is to **examine bias and its role in your work and learning**. Talking about race systematically requires you to examine your lenses and layers. This charge helps us understand that all of our many identities and lived experiences make up the layers we each bring to our instruction. We need to first begin to find the markers of bias in what we believe, how we teach, what we teach, and whom we teach. We have to identify our beliefs, actions, and expectations that impact school and classroom cultures. Only then can we see how this structural racism was built into the system. After we find those markers in our own work, we can start to think about the adaptive and technical shifts that need to happen to make the change we want to see.

In my inaugural principalship in Maryland, I was told at the outset of my assignment that many of the students at my school lived below the poverty line for the county. Just knowing that one fact reinforced a lot of my own biases about my entire student body. To push myself, I rode home one day on the school bus with the kids, and my mouth fell open. The bus stopped at only two apartment buildings, with the remaining stops in communities with single family homes along that route. Many of my students came from two-parent families, and those who didn't had much more care and communal support than I realized—a truth that the story of "below the poverty line" tended to erase. The truth was that I, along with some of my staff, and even, in some cases, my students, had bought into the lie of that story. As a result, my students were showing up to class as the caricatures of the people we told them they were. By no means am I diminishing the economic status of my students and their families or the challenges they faced. They struggled, much as my own mother did raising me in a single-parent home. Yes, the community we served faced economic disenfranchisement that caused trauma, detachment, and fear; however, rather than creating environments that could thwart those factors, we created environments that reacted to and sometimes amplified them. I treated my students like prisoners, made them walk in lines, and created an environment with the intention of "institutionalizing" the students to get them to cooperate. And, perhaps believing they deserved it, my students complied. As Paulo Freire warns against in *Pedagogy of the Oppressed*, I, along with my colleagues in the school system, affirmed our students' identities according to our own biases, beliefs, and assumptions. Luckily, just like in my teaching residency, I have had powerful mentors throughout my life who've pushed me to analyze the why behind the school environment I had helped to create. The experience reminded me that I couldn't just look at data without contending with student identity. As a school leader and as a leader at UnboundEd today, I have had to dig deeper within myself and demand that my staff do the same to eradicate that bias from our work and learning.

The fifth and final charge is to **commit to adaptive change in your teaching and learning**. As we discussed earlier, adaptive change is all about shifting how we think. Mindsets and skill sets must shift simultaneously if we are to have any hope of unwinding the DNA of institutional and systemic racism that plagues the policies, practices, and procedures in our school systems. That adaptive work requires us to honor students' cultural and linguistic identities. If we are to ensure all people have the right to life, liberty, and the pursuit of happiness, if we are to follow our nation's creed of all people being created equal, this final charge is critical. Adaptive shifts are not easy: our institutions, collective communities, and even our own bodies hold the memory of how things were. This kind of change is a constant check and balance of first changing practice and then stepping back to observe and analyze the outcomes to ensure that our students receive a fair opportunity.

These five charges have to sit squarely within the "what" and "how" of teaching and learning. For my colleagues and me at UnboundEd, the five charges support a framework that was created by standing on the shoulders of giants who, over the past many decades, have led the charge for an equitable education and advocated for culturally relevant and responsive pedagogy. Using these charges, we created GLEAM.

Taking Action

When GLEAM™ is exemplified in a student's learning environment, things change. Schools must create a strong culture of achievement and care, a culture strong enough to grow and reinforce a students' academic identities without having to reduce their intrapersonal identities. At their best, schools should hold all students to the same high standards and create an environment that positively affirms all students, including who they are, where they come from, and the multiple languages and vernaculars they speak. That's what Mitchell needed: for his teachers and school leaders to see him fully.

And while Mitchell is one student, he represents so many of the Black, Indigenous, Latinx, Asian American, and other students of color who walk through our classroom doors every day. They are equally deserving of an education that values their wholeness. Our vision is that Black and brown students, all students, get an experience where schools understand the value of looking at who they are, as opposed to what the system is saying. For any student to be successful, we as educators have to examine what our systems are saying, believing, and sustaining around those students. As teachers, we have to examine our actions within that system to create environments in which all students can flourish.

Recognizing the vastness and insidiousness of systemic racism does not render us powerless. Quite the opposite, systems are built to give the results we expect. Our power lies in raising our awareness around the policies, practices, and procedures created to prevent access or support negative beliefs—both implicit and explicit—about students of color and their intellectual capacities. Even when we disaggregate data and it reflects the systems of bias and racism that support low student achievement, we can go on to use that data to craft different results.

Racism has been built through centuries of unexamined bias and power wielded for harm. By ignoring that harm or actively downplaying it as fodder for political campaigns, we are doing detrimental work, not the healing work we hope education will be. Justice in the details is not about avoiding the shame or guilt that may arise when we discuss unexamined racism in our policies, practices, and procedures. As Brené Brown reminds us in her body of work on shame, the only way to extinguish shame is to douse it with empathy and connection. I would respectfully submit that empathy cannot grow without an acknowledgement of the pathology that systemic and structural racism have created within our society. Undoing those structures requires awareness, collective and individual action, and constant readjustment. When we pause to think about our roles in changing these systems, the young people we serve benefit. And understanding ourselves and our systemic roles requires us to examine our lenses and legacies.

4 Legacies and Lenses

When I was a young teacher imagining myself as a role model for my future students, I wasn't always aware of the lenses and legacies informing my teaching. I was not clear that in addition to the education, enthusiasm, and energy I brought to the profession, I also brought baggage, informed both from my own life experiences as well as the many centuries of history that crafted our societal norms and *made* me a Black woman in America. But now, my personal journey and UnboundEd's professional journey toward equity have forced me to reassess some of the moments when I allowed those legacies and lenses to interrupt engaging, affirming, and meaningful educational experiences for students *and* colleagues.

Attending to justice in the details of teaching and learning is just as much about using frameworks to transform our classroom curriculum, planning, and delivery as it is about the difficult, often messy work of understanding our own biases and how they impact every aspect of our personal and professional lives. Whether we are aware of it or not, we teach and lead based on our own personal beliefs, which are informed by both the legacies we inherit and the lenses through which we view the world. UnboundEd's fourth charge asks us to examine bias and its role in our work and learning to better understand how those biases impact the students we teach. Examining our bias leads us to examine the myriad legacies and lenses at the center of decisions we make in our classrooms, staff meetings, and central offices.

Dr. Gloria Ladson-Billings's work points us toward the understanding that in order for curriculum and instruction to shift toward "teaching for social justice," we must first address how we think, or the mindsets we bring into our classrooms as teachers. She writes, "I argue that the first problem teachers confront is believing that successful teaching for poor students of color is primarily about 'what to do.' Instead, I suggest the problem is rooted in how we think—about the social contexts, about the students, about the curriculum, and about instruction."[1] It's a lesson that I've had to learn and relearn throughout my career—that what we see when we walk into a teacher's classroom is an outgrowth of that teacher's mindset.

At the beginning of my career, my experience at Marva Collins Preparatory School made me aware of how my mindset—about what was academically possible for the Black children I wanted to serve—was extremely limited. And in every subsequent teaching experience, I encountered systemic messages that reinforced those limiting views, put me right back at square one of my own internalized bias, and led me to impose those limitations on my students. Before we explore GLEAM™, it's critical that we focus on the mindsets that guide our actions in the classroom. Because if we think of GLEAM or other culturally relevant teaching only as a collection of classroom routines and activities, we will entirely miss the point. And to begin to shift mindsets and ideas, we must first identify their roots in our own lenses, which are informed by our families, communities, and society more broadly.

Like Mitchell's teacher, I also held preconceived notions and assumptions about my students' cultures and the presumed "better way" of other cultural norms. Years ago, I was a co-principal in a fairly large school system in Maryland. Near the end of the school year, we were preparing to celebrate our eighth graders' transition to high school. It was the time of year that is both exhausting and exhilarating. All of us were ready to celebrate: students, teachers, parents, and community members.

As we started preparing for the celebration, I held a meeting with the eighth-grade leadership team members, teachers who were organizing the celebrations, and members of the community. In the past, this annual celebration had been called the "8th Grade Graduation," and both the staff and parents assumed this year would be no different. However, I felt it was my duty to adjust the school's celebration so it fit the system's definition of promotion vs. graduation and what I felt was appropriate for the students in their educational track. In my mind, I thought the community was holding low expectations for our students by calling something as small as an eighth-grade transition ceremony a graduation. To me, it suggested we had to celebrate now because students may not make it to the actual graduation. I informed everyone we would *not* be calling it a graduation. Rather, an event like this could only officially be called a promotion ceremony.

When I made the announcement, everyone—teachers, parents, community members, and likely students when they heard—was angry. I was met with a chorus of "How dare you?" and "Ms. Robinson, we don't want to call it a promotion; it's a graduation." But I was adamant. I let them all know that there are only two institutions you graduate from: high school and college. I thought the pushback was unwarranted. They would say to me, "Ms. Robinson it *is* a graduation, and I don't know when my child will hear those words again. I want to be able to celebrate it with them."

I was ready for that. I would quip back, "Is that the only expectation you have for your student? Just that he graduate from eighth grade?"

Until one day, a parent showed up at my door, furious. She walked right up to me and said, "Do you see me? Do you *see* me? You're not even from this community. You don't know what we go through." She made me realize I really hadn't been listening. But still, I dug in my heels and forced everyone to call it an eighth-grade promotion.

You see, when I was initially offered the position of co-leading the middle school, I was not only briefed on the abysmal academic progress the school was known for, but also about the crime, trauma, and systemic environmental issues that poured in from the surrounding neighborhood.

When the district leaders handed me the keys to the building, they said, "We just want you to go in and get the murder rate down." I was shocked. It was clear they believed that somehow my racial identity, along with my skill and sheer will, would not only eradicate the academic decline—an implicit message not included in the directive with the keys—but fix all the social and emotional outcomes for students and their community. I immediately felt two stings: one of the low expectations they held for the students and the community, and another of pressure as a Black educated woman, who now held the responsibility of righting the wrongs built over decades of injustice. But like many neophyte leaders who led with their ego, I accepted the offer. I took that entire responsibility solely on my own shoulders, with all of the overwhelming pressure and expectations that came with it. The argument of "graduation" vs. "promotion" became a battleground for that ego-driven charge.

It wasn't until I left the system—for an opportunity to coach and support leaders who were in schools similar to the one I had led—that I finally, *finally* understood what that mother had been trying to say to me when she came to my door. She and the other parents were trying to tell me that they wanted to honor this moment of celebration with their children, because it was a real and valid feeling (one I had dismissed) and they did not know if a moment like that would come again. They were saying very clearly that surviving in an environment so deeply impacted by oppressive systems, even just to the eighth grade, was a success that should not be glossed over or ignored.

When I stopped and examined my own beliefs, two things became clear. First, I had significant room to grow in what I knew and understood about my own perception of low-income communities. It was Paulo Freire's *Pedagogy of the Oppressed*—which so clearly defines the roles of the oppressor and the oppressed—that opened my eyes to the hidden beliefs driving the decisions around systems of housing, school zoning, and services. Second, my beliefs about teachers, students, and communities as well as the assimilationist values I held, had played into how I led and supported my school.

It didn't matter that I was a Black woman, raised by a single mother who sometimes struggled to provide the best life for her girls. It didn't matter that I had taught in districts all over the country by that point. With all of those experiences, my deep love for our students, and my pedagogical knowledge—even with all of that—as a Black woman, I had doubled down on shaming and othering the predominantly Black community my school served. Instead of honoring the traditions of that community, I pushed an assimilationist lens that only served to uphold a completely made-up standard that was divorced from my students' lived experiences. I failed to see that I could continue to demand and expect excellence, while also sharing in the celebration of my students' accomplishment. Instead, I had expected an entire community to bend to *my* understanding and to *my* cultural lenses for what their celebration should be.

Understanding Legacies

To deliver pedagogy that is liberating, expansive, and rigorous, and for any students to be successful, we as educators must examine our role in the systems that impact our lives and the lives of our students.

Legacies are ideas, values, beliefs that are built on our ancestors' experiences. Legacies are passed down, filtered, and adapted through the years according to circumstances and environment, but continuing at their core to inform our beliefs and behaviors in the present. Legacies are the many historical markers in this country that have defined how we think about our fellow humans, where we place people in our social hierarchies, how we acquire land, the barriers we create to bringing people into our country, and how we require them to assimilate. These legacies impact the layers of our identities. Layers include aspects of our social identity such as race, gender, level of education, socioeconomic status, religion, and more. Both legacies and the layers they create inform the lenses we bring to our lives and work. The lenses that influence perception are inextricably shaped by historical legacies and layers.

None of us enjoy an unbiased lens in any aspect of our lives, in part because there are legacies informing our beliefs in ways that are impossible to see clearly in every immediate and daily interaction. Our success in unbraiding the complex and troubled strands of this country's educational legacy depends on our ability to notice and disrupt the individual and collective lenses through which we view our students and others. I have recently had to come to terms with the many familial ancestors and historical figures who have played a role in the story of Black people's existence in this country. I now believe it is just as essential to examine Thomas Jefferson, William Wilberforce, and the like's influence on thought as much as it is to consider Harriet Tubman, Paul Laurence Dunbar, Ida B. Wells, Dr. Martin Luther King, and many other sheroes and heroes who have been placed in my lexicon of Black history. All of these influencers play a role in how I am viewed, how my race was crafted in this country, and my access to opportunity and education. And if I'm honest, their thinking and writing has impacted how I viewed myself, my students, and the ways I've provided or supported instruction—both in positive and negative ways.

A few years ago, I argued with a fellow educator and well-known policy leader about the literary canon. When we talked about rethinking ELA curricula for Black and brown students, he was insistent that students *must* read books like *To Kill a Mockingbird* and *The Catcher in the Rye*. I was clear with him that while I wanted students to read those books, I also wanted them to read *Roll of Thunder, Hear My Cry,* and Toni Morrison's *Song of Solomon*. Like many other educators across the country, I wanted us to expand the idea of the literary canon. I asked him as he defended the need to read these "classics," exactly "Who gets to decide what is a classic? And classic to whom?" My point then, and now, is that our classroom practices—and our own mindsets about those practices—require examination, if only to just unearth the legacies and lenses that inform them.

What Are Lenses?

I have been writing about the lenses through which we view the world, and they are really made up of the many layers and legacies that we carry with us. These layers and legacies aren't just moments that we tuck away somewhere, never to be seen again. No, layers and legacies inform the various lenses that shape the policies, practices, and procedures dictating every aspect of our real lives.

At UnboundEd, we rely in part on Mark A. Williams's work[2] to help us uncover the many lenses operating in our everyday lives and—by extension—our classrooms. Williams outlines 10 lenses: Assimilationist, Colorblind, Cultural Centrist, Elitist, Integrationist,

Meritocratic, Multiculturalist, Seclusionist, Transcendent, and
Victim/Caretaker. As we considered our equity journey as individuals
within UnboundEd, we realized we needed to have a reference point,
a document to help our staff and the teachers we work with to
uncover their own lenses and layers, which is why we created the
Anti-Bias Toolkit a few years ago. It is a practical guide for educators
that goes into greater detail on how or why each lens is important to
explore for your own personal growth and equity journey. We will
reference the toolkit often throughout this book and guide you to it
when there are ideas or concepts worth examining more closely.
However, in this chapter, I will focus on just three lenses referenced in
the toolkit: Assimilationist, Meritocratic, and Colorblind. I've chosen
these three lenses to highlight because they are so pronounced in our
modern national discourse about education.

When I recall that eighth-grade promotion ceremony, I am
acutely aware that my assimilationist lens was in full effect.
Assimilation requires everyone to "Adopt the values, customs, and
language of the dominant culture."[3] In this case, the dominant culture
was the school district's policies and norms, which differed from those
of my school's community. I assumed that the district's way—because
that way was validated by whiteness and power—was the better way,
and so I dismissed the voices of teachers, parents, and community
members who were trying to tell me that their traditions, values, and
celebrations were more important than an edict issued from on high.
My assimilationist lens is perhaps the one I have worked hardest to
unravel throughout my career. An assimilationist lens both allowed
my family and me to navigate racist systems *and* caused harm to the
communities I've worked to support as an educator.

I was raised in Ohio by a single mother, alongside my maternal
grandparents and my extended family, both paternal and maternal.
That upbringing provided my first lenses through which to perceive
both myself and the world outside of my tight-knit family.

My mother's parents hailed from the Deep South; they migrated from Georgia and Tennessee to Ohio in the late 1940s. Legacies of brutal Jim Crow segregation forced my maternal grandparents to leave their homes, seeking better opportunities and the assurance that *all* their children would have access to an education beyond what they had received. The lenses they developed growing up in the South during Jim Crow laws, and through their Great Depression journey, formed the survival tactics they would instill in their growing family.

For many Black people in that generation, the migration north into factory towns meant shedding our provincial identity and acquiring a new one in the big city (regardless of how small that town or city actually was). For my maternal family, that meant having a consistent job and raising children who would—without question—attend school. Their children would not be plagued with the experiences they had known: not having enough money to purchase shoes to walk to school, or sacrificing weekly earnings to pay a poll tax. Both of these realities played a role in my grandmother's illiteracy, which was a societal neglect she was determined to spare my mother and her siblings from. Education in the North meant my mom and her siblings would learn to read, write, and calculate their future. More importantly, it meant my grandparents could give their children the same opportunities they had watched their white neighbors take for granted in the South. So you see, the anti-literacy laws we discussed in Chapter 1 are the legacy that caused my maternal grandmother's illiteracy, which became a layer of her identity that made donning an assimilationist lens so very important to her when she moved her family north. In my upbringing, this meant my own lenses were deeply colored by my family's desire to assimilate into the pathways available to white people.

Assimilation became the lens through which I funneled most of my elementary and secondary education experience. My mom was certain that if her daughters practiced the right intonation of voice, had the right hairstyles and clothes, they could never be shut out of any opportunities to further their education and life trajectories. Of course, that "rightness" was centered around white-dominant cultural norms. My mother witnessed first-hand the deterioration—from the training level of the staff to the access to high-quality materials—that began to happen in the neighborhood schools that were predominately Black in the South. Armed with that information, she decided to move to a suburb of Dayton, Ohio, that we subsequently integrated in the 1980s.

From the first to fourth grade, other than my sister and me, there was only one other family of color whose kids attended our school. I was chased home regularly by the white kids and faced years of micro- and macroaggressions from white teachers, students, and their families in both my classrooms and neighborhood. My mother made sure we socialized with our Black family and friends and spent the summers at a camp that was mostly made up of children of color, so as to balance our "all white" schooling experience. And yet, when my mom then moved us to Akron, Ohio, at the onset of my fifth-grade year, and I walked into my first classroom with a Black teacher and other Black students, I was scared. It didn't matter that my mother had made conscious decisions in an attempt to counterbalance the realities of assimilation, to instill Black Pride into us on a daily basis in our upbringing. On the whole, the idea I was taught—both directly and indirectly from the schoolhouse as well as what the media portrayed—was that Black culture was less valuable. I internalized a message that Black people were scary and dangerous. This lens had long-lasting implications.

As educators, when we encounter children who haven't previously or fully assimilated into those systems, we are trained to force them into a cultural way of being that is often foreign to them. Even as a Black woman, I too am guilty of negatively framing my students and the communities from which they come. That framing is informed by the lenses that shaped my own education via perspectives and entrenched systems that othered both my culture and my implicit ways of knowing. I was made to believe that the further I was able to assimilate, the more I could attain in terms of academic accomplishments and, ultimately, my career and income trajectory. It was why I saw myself so clearly in Mitchell when I visited his classroom. Just as Mitchell's ways of knowing were silenced by his teacher, mine had been silenced by years of a similar education, which led me, in turn, to silence the cultural and linguistic knowledge of my students and their families. It would take decades for me to fully identify my assimilationist lens and begin the work of dismantling its impact on my life and work.

The assimilationist lens operates at all levels of the education system. And many educators of color, to gain professional success, had to assimilate to white cultural norms in large and small ways, even as they felt the daily and flattening crush of that lens. In turn, we push our students to assimilate because we also want them to enjoy similar "success," even though we know the cost. It would be naïve of me to not acknowledge that assimilating—or gaining dominant narrative knowledge—supported my academic and professional careers. However, that assimilationist lens did little to disrupt the status quo or ensure that future students would face a different reality.

I now believe that, as educators, we should name and discuss assimilation with students as they progress in their education, acknowledging that there is a dominant culture and understanding what and how assimilation works in our culture. Students should be made aware of, and understand, when assimilation is at play. This will, at the very least, allow children to stand firm in who they are and to make decisions to circumvent or assimilate into the dominant society.

Lisa Delpit reminds us: "If you are not already a participant in the culture of power, being told explicitly the rules of that culture makes acquiring power easier."[4] It is imperative that we teach students that assimilation can be a tool used to navigate spaces, but it should not be a means to replace who they are or devalue their own identities or cultures. I, by no means, want to cheer-lead assimilation writ large, but rather I want to acknowledge that students may need to traverse current structures even as they work to change them.

Which leads us to the meritocratic lens. **Meritocracy** has deep roots in our national mythology and storytelling. We are told over and over again that those who work hard reap the rewards of that hard work. Similarly, we are told that when people do not succeed, when they fail, when they live in poverty, and when they are homeless, it is because they did not work hard enough. We assume that successful people are smarter than us, more savvy than us, and work harder than us. And, of course, we confer all of the opposite imagery, values, and characteristics on people we deem unsuccessful: laziness, lack of intelligence, and an inability to navigate the world. Meritocracy feeds assimilation, because when people live outside of the powerful norm that is whiteness and wealth in our country, we demand that they shrink and distort themselves to adopt the values we believe they lack. Essentially, our meritocratic lens determines which groups of people we believe deserve things in this country.

Take for instance the college admissions scandal of 2019,[5] also known as Operation Varsity Blues. Wealthy and famous parents from across the country paid for their children's undue admission into prestigious colleges like Yale or the University of Southern California. This organized and systematic gaming of college admissions hinged on one key lens: meritocracy. Unlike the many Black and brown teenagers or those teenagers living in poverty who apply to these colleges and universities each year, the mostly white, very affluent participants in this scandal were perceived by school selection committees as deserving their place. This believed deservedness is what allowed the charade to continue for as long and as widely as it did. If a poor, Afro-Latinx kid from Milwaukee had suddenly been admitted to USC on a sports scholarship for a sport they never played, their perceived lack of merit would have immediately been cause for further scrutiny. In fact, just a few years before the 2019 scandal, a case about affirmative action made it all the way to the U.S. Supreme Court, powered by the argument that Abby Fisher,[6] a white applicant to the University of Texas, had lost her admissions spot to people less deserving than herself. Ultimately, the Supreme Court ruled in favor of The University of Texas, invalidating Ms. Fisher's argument.

In K–12 education, there are numerous examples of how meritocracy is reinforced. I have subscribed to this lens more times than I can remember, even when I knew that that lens was not an accurate reflection of how the world works. In most schools in which I have worked, we have used a meritocratic lens; because allegedly "the cream always rises to the top," we base our school behavior plan and community policies on what we perceive an individual student's initiative, competence, and accomplishments to be. We tell students, "If you have abilities and you work hard enough, you can compete with anyone and make all your dreams come true." We remind them, "If you have enough grit, you can make it."

In reality, when you're a Black male in a classroom and you tower over the teacher, it doesn't matter how much grit or potential you have if your teacher views you as a threat. When you're a young immigrant girl whose district does not provide adequate ELL resources, it doesn't matter how hard-working you are, if your school does not support you. If you're a student whose teacher does not see you as a valuable person in your school community, you may not see yourself or your peers as inherently valuable. I believe that too often we uphold grit rather than encourage agency. Rewarding grit means that I, as an educator, don't have to change my beliefs about you, the student, even when those beliefs are informed by harmful layers and legacies.

For me, as an educator, to help build your agency instead, I have to change my beliefs about what you can do. I have to challenge my own lenses as well as the legacies that shape them. I have to understand that our country's policies, structures, and rhetorical flourishes lauding grit as the one determining factor in success, in fact dismiss the powerful lenses making true meritocracy impossible. Prioritizing agency instead of grit is one way we disrupt the lens of meritocracy in our classrooms. When a young man of color is primed to activate his own agency of his learning, then a failing mark on a quiz or assessment does not become a plot on his educational trajectory, rather it is feedback on what unfinished learning he may need to unearth to understand the standard, skill, and/or concept being assessed. Jeff Howard consistently reminds us, in his formidable work at the Efficacy Institute, "that failure is feedback" and the efficacy principle that development means getting stronger and better at whatever endeavor you are trying to obtain is pertinent to a student's development of their agency.

The fact is that grade-level, engaging, affirming, and meaningful instruction is already happening in thousands of classrooms across the country. However, most of the students who receive a grade-level, engaging, affirming, and meaningful—GLEAM—education on a daily basis are white, affluent, or both. Our society believes those students have earned and are more deserving of this type of instruction. To upend our meritocratic lens, we must really push ourselves to reconsider who is deserving of GLEAM instruction. The answer *should* be *every* student.

Finally, we've talked before about a colorblind lens. **Colorblindness** is a refusal to acknowledge race or ethnicity. This lens often disguises itself by saying, "Everyone should be treated as a unique individual."[7] Mitchell's teacher shared her belief in the merits of colorblindness. She thought that not acknowledging Mitchell's race would build a better classroom experience for him and her other students of color. But all colorblindness did was to obscure the bias that she brought into her interactions with students and to ignore the cultural and linguistic experiences of Mitchell and his peers. Her colorblindness was a barrier to equality in her classroom.

Colorblindness is also a lens that compounds assimilation and meritocracy. When we pretend that race is not a factor in students' lives, we are asking them, at best, to assimilate their cultures or, at worst, erase them. We are demanding that they bury or hide their cultural differences to fuel our vision of a dominant culture. Similarly, when colorblindness and meritocracy meet, we refuse to acknowledge that race informs who we think is deserving. We ignore the opportunities given to one racial group at the expense of the other and then assign negative attributes to students whose educational trajectory is stalled by their lack of access to grade-level, engaging, affirming, and meaningful instruction.

As we continue to really look at how our lenses impact our classrooms, I invite you to ask yourself: What lenses do I hold? Where did these lenses begin to form? Is there a healthier version of them? And finally: How can we widen our own apertures and challenge the lenses that cause harm to ourselves and our students? The answer to so many of these questions requires us to dig deep into the historical legacies that drive our understanding of the world.

This is not to suggest that we immediately destroy or deny our lenses once we begin to see how they color our perception. The many lenses we bring to our classrooms are also what have allowed us to survive and thrive at different points in our lives. The assimilationist lens passed down from my grandparents, to my mother, and then to me had a place and a function in my family's survival through Jim Crow into the present. Similarly, there are times, when assimilating to a particular cultural norm or practice is beneficial without being problematic. However, interrogating our lenses requires us to assess when they show up, how we are utilizing them, and if those lenses cause harm or reinforce a negative societal order for students. Approaching our lenses with a critical eye also allows us to determine when those lenses are no longer useful and when we can release them in our pursuit of justice.

The Foundation for Equitable Education

As educators, the work of identifying and transforming our mindsets is the only foundation on which we can build equitable education. Finding justice in the details of teaching and learning does not begin until we start with unraveling our legacies, layers, and lenses to support our students in doing the same. Again, Dr. Ladson-Billings's words ring true here, "Teachers who I term *culturally relevant* assume that an asymmetrical (even antagonistic) relationship exists between poor students of color and society. Thus, their vision of their work is one of preparing students to combat inequity by being highly competent and critically conscious."[8]

Our current educational discourse suggests that culturally relevant pedagogy/teaching (CRP/T) is a new concept, used in the last few decades to reverse detrimental literacy and learning trends for Black students as well as other students of color. However, history teaches us that culturally relevant pedagogy is not new; more importantly, it is a powerful dismantling tool because at the core, it is about the academic achievement of Black and brown students. Black educators during Reconstruction who were teaching in schools, basements, churches, and even fields were building a cultural fabric with which to help make literacy relevant for newly freed Black people. In building multigenerational classroom environments, they were harnessing the power of community and love to fast-track their students' learning— and it worked. The exponential literacy and educational gains Black educators shepherded immediately after the end of 250 years of chattel slavery were astounding. Those educators predated GLEAM by 150 years, but their success hinged on their rootedness in community as well as their belief in their students' brilliance and ultimate success.

After decades of studying and writing about CRP/T, by 2014, Dr. Ladson-Billings had become so disenchanted by what was being passed off as culturally relevant pedagogy that she published *Culturally Relevant Pedagogy 2.0: a.k.a. The Remix*,[9] where she made it clear that what is being called culturally relevant pedagogy is often a distortion and corruption of the ideas she attempted to promulgate in her original work. According to Paris and Alim in 2017, cultural relevance has become akin to cultural voyeurism whereby educators use vestiges of pop culture and hip-hop to hook kids only to revert to their traditional forms of pedagogy. There's more to CRP/T than merely playing the latest song and attempting to speak the way you hear your students speak. And it certainly is not mimicking what you may have "learned" from visiting a Black church or other sacred Black space, which is not necessarily religious. But it is a place where Black people are free from the "white gaze."[10]

Our nation's legacies on race determine how we have historically conceptualized and implemented CRP/T. When every race but white is viewed as the other, we are taught that to get "those kids" to succeed we must learn the language of the other—an idea that is reduced to the basest parts of racial and cultural understanding. This lack of understanding stems from an overarching ignorance about people of color and how they view education. There is a common belief that only certain people of color care about the education of their children while others do not. There is also a particular, nearly singular perspective on how families should exhibit educational care for their children. Such notions involve being able to attend school meetings, in-person during school hours, and school functions held during school hours, and volunteering at school during school hours. Little consideration is given to families whose schedules and lives do not fit this model.

When we interrogate our own legacies, layers, and lenses, we have a new foundation upon which to ask important questions, including: Who is this model built for? Can families without a parent staying home and another parent working outside the home navigate their children's education with equal ease? If not, will the school community work to accommodate and include them, or will it dismiss them as disengaged or apathetic parents? How have working styles and family structures changed since a particular policy or system was created? Are we punishing parents and families for whom this model might not work? How can we eliminate the vestiges of a society that devalues a global majority in our school building?

With this as our starting point, we can begin to rebuild our classroom practices so they are grade-level, engaging, (culturally and identity) affirming, and meaningful. Now, we can begin the work of GLEAM.

5 Overview of GLEAM

shared earlier that at the beginning of my career as an educator,
I didn't always understand myself as a practitioner of teaching.
Before I officially entered the field and before my Marva Collins
Preparatory experience, I believed my greatest role in my classroom
was that of a role model. This belief was a by-product both of my
own assimilationist lens and of the national rhetoric around the
teaching profession. Throughout my own life and education, I had
heard teachers most often discussed as caring, impactful, selfless,
and many other adjectives (which, of course, they are!), but these
descriptors had little to do with their skillfulness, their knowledge of
craft, or their brilliance. So it made a lot of sense that I thought my
most important task as a teacher was to provide Black and brown
children with more examples of Black adults who had learned the
"code" of success.

As I do the work of constantly peeling back the legacies, layers, and
lenses that inform my biased thinking, I am also committed to
cultivating a mindset within myself and other educators of being skilled
education practitioners. *Justice is found in the details of teaching and
learning*® comes both through that rigorous, ongoing self-evaluation,

and an investment in craft. Pursuing justice in our craft requires orienting ourselves toward growth and ensuring every student who passes through our classrooms has an equitable chance at not only succeeding in school but also in developing the skills they need to thrive.

In addition to being greatly influenced by Dr. Gloria Ladson-Billings, other thought leaders, researchers, and practitioners like Dr. Lisa Delpit have supported the evolution of thought needed to stand up the GLEAM™ framework I first mentioned in Chapter 3. In her article "The Silenced Dialogue," Dr. Delpit saliently reminds us that, ". . . students must be *taught* the codes needed to participate fully in the mainstream of American life, not by being forced to attend to hollow, inane, decontextualized subskills, but rather within the context of meaningful communicative endeavors [and learning]; . . . they must be allowed the resource of the teacher's expert knowledge, while being helped to acknowledge their own "expertness." . . ."[1]

When I first read this excerpt, I felt a wind of freedom coming from its acknowledgment; someone recognized a dialogue that was often silenced in my experience. She expressed what I had felt and seen, that students who hail from white or affluent households—whose home lives and daily experiences are grounded in dominant culture—enter into our schools with what I believed, and still believe, are two major advantages. They either enter with the organic inheritance of privilege or dominant cultural currency, sometimes both. It is with these two advantages on which scholars, leaders, and yes, we teachers, often stand and don't share access to, which sideswipe or thwart direct and explicit instruction.

Of this, Dr. Delpit says, "But parents who don't function within that culture [of power] often want something else. . . . They want to ensure that the school provides their children with discourse patterns, interactional styles, and spoken and written language codes that will allow them success in the larger society."[2] Our classrooms often proceed without acknowledging that all children need exposure to the dominant culture's language (both spoken and written), while honoring and utilizing their own local and historical cultural and linguistic context to support learning.

Dr. Delpit's message rang true for me as a learner and a teacher. My mother had given me her lessons on dominant culture norms to ensure I would push against what she knew to be the explicit and implicit bias in expectations my teachers held. My mom's lessons came from her own book of life lessons, with the chapter title, "You need to have the power of their language and know their social norms, so you can be successful in their world." This one is a lesson that many families of color teach their children. Unfortunately for my mom and many other parents, that particular lesson proves ineffective against entrenched and inequitable systems. Studies of racial economic gaps are tangible proof that working twice as hard might land you a degree or career positioning, but historical government and economic decisions add the invisible hurdles that Black and brown families and individuals are far and few to overcome.

I think often about those hurdles—both in society as well as in the school I co-led—and my first attempts at trying to hoist my middle school students over them. My immediate default was creating school policies, practices, and procedures that demanded assimilation, without the acknowledgment of the intent. That default orientation toward assimilation seemed to creep in without me even being aware. It caused me to judge my students and families, and locked me into playing a role of pied piper: if they would only follow my assimilationist rules, they too could get out, get ahead, and overcome. The more my students and their families resisted my efforts, the more agitated and judgmental I became about them. That misguided judgment haunts me to this day.

The truth is that if my students were behind academically, our teachers were behind pedagogically. While most of the teachers on our school's staff were fully committed to supporting our students in academic and social growth, the majority of them were new to the education profession. Many were graduate students who had joined alternative teaching programs that promised a graduate degree if they held teaching positions while continuing their education. When my professional panic set in as a principal in Maryland, I scheduled leadership retreats where we combined work on belief systems with professional development in technical leadership. Mantras and rituals were created so that our students would begin to see themselves as scholars. But even with all of these carefully crafted systems, we were still losing our footing as we fumbled in getting our staff and scholars on paths to career and college readiness.

Despite my best efforts, I lacked what we here at UnboundEd now call a GLEAM lens. Eventually, instead of doubling down on assimilation, I began to accept Dr. Delpit's whole message and solution: that students could and should be co-authors in their own learning and in devising their own path forward. That transformation allowed me to understand that co-authorship allows us as educators to name the dominant cultural lenses that exist in learning and allow students to understand the role those lenses play in how we understand academic achievement and college and career readiness. Co-authorship also provides the space for students to bring their whole selves to learning: their language and vernacular, local and historical contexts, and individual and cultural identities. Out of this newfound understanding and belief in co-authorship, the GLEAM lens was born.

In a lot of ways, I see Dr. Delpit and Dr. Gloria Ladson-Billings as two of my scholarly godmothers in my educational journey and certainly as people whose research informed our GLEAM framework. In her 2006 essay "Yes, But How Do We Do It?," Dr. Ladson-Billings talks about the industry that arose around her work documenting educators whose Black and brown students were excelling academically.

She writes, "Unfortunately, much of the work that addresses successful teaching of poor students of color is linked to the notion of the teacher as heroic isolate. Thus, stories such as those of Marva Collins, Jaime Escalante, Vivian Paley, and LouAnne Johnson inadvertently transmit a message of the teacher as savior and charismatic maverick without exploring the complexities of teaching and nuanced intellectual work that undergirds pedagogical practices."[3] In my keynotes, I too call teachers superheroes—in the context that those characters are constantly putting the greater good before their own—and while I deeply believe this, I also know that "heroic isolates" as Dr. Ladson-Billings calls them, are not a systemic solution to the racism inherent to our education system.

Dr. Ladson-Billings is hesitant to give educators an easy how-to on culturally relevant instruction, and so am I. Part of this hesitation, at least for me, comes from my deep belief in the professional capacity of educators. When doctors train to heal people, it is impossible that in their many years of school and internship they will see every possible scenario, because each patient and each context for that patient is different. Similarly, lawyers are not trained down to the letter of each case they will ever encounter. Instead, they are given a thorough understanding of how the law works and asked to apply that understanding to a range of possible real-life scenarios. For many reasons that are influenced by the historical legacies of this country, we do not often talk about doctors, teachers, and lawyers in the same breath. This does not mean teachers are any less thoughtful professionals or skilled practitioners. So it's just as important that educators be armed with a plethora of concepts, pedagogy, and context to know what tools to pull up, not only drawing on grade-level expectations, but also allowing students to be at the center of learning.

As we explore GLEAM, I hope you will understand it as a framework for developing your teaching practice and your equity lens. That's because I believe a how-to guide alone is not enough to honor the many contexts in which you all are teaching and leading. A step-by-step guide is not conducive to the kind of flexibility and agility you need as a teacher or leader to best serve the young people who come through your classroom doors each day. Instead, GLEAM is a framework that helps you orient yourself, your classrooms, and your systems toward educational justice. It sharpens your lens toward recalibration and reorientation of curriculum and instruction without providing you a concrete list of dos and don'ts. It is not meant to be a scripted inflexible process, but rather one that serves as a scaffold to support internalizing a new mindset, lens, and approach to classroom planning, with GLEAM instruction in mind.

I also acknowledge that our students' learning cannot wait for a massive overhaul of curriculum and materials. The GLEAM framework is meant to support us as we navigate the justice in the details *right now*, regardless of where your district or state is in the adoption process. It is our hope that GLEAM becomes both the primary framing in our discussions of pedagogy, planning, and execution of lessons as well as a lens educators can utilize in assessing and analyzing student data.

As Alice Wiggins, Vice President for Instructional Design at UnboundEd, says, "When we distill culturally relevant teaching down to a set of practices, strategies, procedures, mnemonics, and such, we miss the essence and the intent of culturally relevant instruction. So our conception of GLEAM doesn't stop with grade-level, engaging, affirming, and meaningful practices." This is not to say that, at UnboundEd, we don't suggest or even advocate for specific practices that help bring about effective instruction. It's just that these practices are complex. They often require layering with one another and can be applied differently according to circumstance and student needs. Our choices about when and how to use them are mediated by our mindsets about students, about schools, and about ourselves.

GLEAM, like much of culturally relevant and responsive teaching and learning, is on a continuum; at any given moment in the planning and execution of learning, the practitioner *and* students are somewhere in the progression, working toward GLEAM.

Developing GLEAM

When I think about the birth of GLEAM, I remember sitting in a conference room in 2017 with a colleague who, at the time, led UnboundEd's research and evaluation work. I was going into detail about my experience as a resident teacher at the Marva Collins Preparatory School. I shared how quickly I began to realize that teaching wasn't just about the materials or content and not only about the teachers' and leaders' expectations. My experience at Marva Collins taught me that great teaching lies in the details, the careful consideration of our students: who they are and who they can become.

As my colleague began to ask me questions about those details, I named examples. First, the standard of learning for the students at Marva Collins Preparatory School was unequivocally at or above their combined grade levels; if the students were to compete and succeed in class, they needed to not only meet grade-level expectations but also, if possible, exceed them. Second, the teachers and school leader held high expectations for students' learning, while at the same time acknowledging any missing prerequisites and figuring out the just-in-time scaffolds—necessary to get students to their learning goals. Many of those scaffolds hold culturally responsive and sustaining tenets. Third, although my internship predated the academic standards we use today, the teachers at Marva Collins Preparatory School used curriculum guides and always planned with the current and next grade level in mind. They allowed students to sit in the tension of concepts or ideas that were new and challenging. Studies show that vigorous and productive struggle in learning literally grows neurons and dendrites in the brain;[4] I believe if we'd had the means of magnifying those students' brains at Marva Collins, they would look like dendrite gardens!

Because students at Marva Collins were engaged in rigorous learning, there was a constant flow of "Yes, this is hard but you can do it!" and "Okay, you made a mistake, but we will not let you fail!" or "Yes, your learning is ultimately your responsibility, but we are in this together." These mindsets and affirmations were necessary to uphold the productive struggle that students needed to move through the learning. The school's mantras, collaborative classroom chants, and constant flow of encouragement from the teachers were all a central part of the environment. The final example of those details in great teaching came from the first day of my internship I mentioned earlier, when I observed students participating in meaningful conversation about George Orwell's *Animal Farm*. I sat in awe as the teacher drew on the students' knowledge of their immediate local and historical cultural context to teach them the advanced text.

By the end of my conversation with my colleague at UnboundEd, on the other side of a whole swipe board and numerous pages of notes, my colleague and I had planted and cultivated the seeds of GLEAM. The nuanced intellectual work discussed by Dr. Ladson-Billings, Dr. Lisa Delpit, Dr. Django Paris, Dr. Geneva Gay, Zaretta Hammond, Dr. Beverly Tatum, and many more requires understanding our own legacies, layers, and lenses to provide GLEAM instruction. Our hypothesis is that only when mindset and planning are purposefully put into service of grade-level, engaging, affirming, and meaningful instruction do we see the kinds of teacher actions and student experiences that exemplify culturally relevant teaching, or what I hope becomes the standard for good teaching. As we explore GLEAM further together, we will uncover more of the mindsets that must shift for our classrooms to truly become engines of justice in the details.

Shifting Mindsets

For many of us, our teacher training imparted the unproductive mindset that our primary task in a classroom is to manage bodies and maintain order. Historical legacies, those that code the bodies of Black, Indigenous, and brown people as needing constant correction, mean that students like Mitchell across the country are more often disciplined rather than engaged in their classrooms. Instead, a productive mindset is one that encourages you as an educator to operate with informed empathy and to build a learning partnership with students that does not excuse students from working hard to pursue excellence.

In Mitchell's classroom, his teacher partnered with Thanh when he interjected and added Vietnamese to the story reading. She understood that helping Thanh bridge the gap between her story, told in English, to the goats on his grandmother's farm would build his engagement in the lesson and expand other students' learning as well. Moving away from managing bodies and maintaining order means extending the opportunity for similar partnerships to all of our students. Doing this doesn't strip away rigor in our classroom—a fallacy we are often taught to believe, especially in classrooms with predominantly Black and brown students—instead, it offers the opportunity for students to become the owners of their learning.

Moving away from a dynamic of control also means we have to believe that our students are filled with possibilities; they are not empty vessels we must fill. Every last child who comes through our classroom doors, comes not only with a cultural and familial understanding of the world, but also with their own thoughts, wonderings, and experiences. We can only build culturally relevant and affirming curricula when we acknowledge that reality and build in room for the infinite possibilities they bring to school.

Perhaps one of the most unproductive mindsets we as educators must shift away from on the way to finding justice in the details of teaching and learning is the idea that the curriculum we teach is somehow an ideologically neutral document. As Dr. Ladson-Billings reminds us, a school curriculum is a cultural artifact, which is a reality I was learning when my colleagues and I at UnboundEd began to conceive of GLEAM. As educators we affirm our students' identities in the curriculum we choose. GLEAM can help us to understand how to provide a curriculum that is *just,* one that dismantles systemic racism rather than supports it. Knowing what we do now about the numerous legacies, lenses, and layers we each bring to our work every day, it is impossible to imagine that curriculum could possibly be neutral or "objective," and yet this idea is a refrain echoed in our schools and districts regularly.

When we acknowledge that there is an "asymmetrical (even antagonistic) relationship between poor students of color and society"—a relationship that is encoded into our policies, practices, and procedures—we begin to shift into a productive mindset. This new mindset allows us to understand that, as a product of the many oppressive systems our students face, we *must* deconstruct and reconstruct[5] curriculum according to the needs and identities of the students we serve. Challenging curricula allows us to support students in developing the various skills they need to better understand and critique their social position and context *and* to create opportunities for students to see themselves reflected and affirmed in what they are learning.

Unproductive mindsets often arise from our lack of exposure to diverse identities and ideas. Dr. Beverly Tatum, in her book *Why Are All the Black Kids Still Sitting Together in the Cafeteria?* notes our limited exposure to other people and cultures. "According to a 2013 American Values Survey conducted by the Public Research Institute (PRRI), the social networks of White people in the United States are very homogenous. Indeed, the PRRI researchers found that 75 percent of Whites have entirely White social networks, without any minority presences."[6] These realities fuel some of our most unproductive mindsets. If you are interested in exploring more about productive and unproductive classroom mindsets, the UnboundEd Anti-Bias toolkit goes into greater depth (you can find the link at the end of this book). But the most crucial piece to understand is that to begin to *shift* these ideas and ways of thinking, we must first identify their roots in our own lenses, lenses informed by our families, communities, and society more broadly and then focus on counteracting them.

And so this brings us back to GLEAM and its purpose: to actively work together as an educator community to dismantle our own biases and unproductive mindsets. That work drives us toward our goal of eliminating the predictability of student achievement by race and low-economic status by providing Grade-Level, Engaging, Affirming, and Meaningful instruction. When talking about GLEAM, we center students of color so that we collectively focus on dismantling systems of disenfranchisement. We focus on the students who have historically been pushed to the margins in order for all students to benefit and thrive.

GLEAM: Grade-Level, Engaging, Affirming, and Meaningful

Grade-level means that when equitable instruction is the focus, curriculum, texts, and other resources in use by the teacher will be of high quality and will consistently match the level of cognitive complexity demanded by the standards of that particular grade. Real benefits and opportunities for growth come from bringing students to the work of their grade level, and high-quality curricular materials adopted at the school level can help ensure success for any students with unfinished learning. Grade-level learning is for *all* students to have access to, not just the students who we, as educators, deem ready. In focusing on grade-level instruction, we highlight acceleration[7] as a strategy that can support all student populations. I recognize that some students in special education may require additional support or accommodations. But I also think it's important to recognize that acceleration, rather than only remediation, is a critical strategy. It's important as educators that we are always pushing for exposure to grade-level standards, context, and concepts.

As an educator, delivering grade-level instruction also means you have to become intimately familiar with the expectations students should have met in their previous grade *and* understand how what they learn in your classroom prepares them for work in the subsequent grade. How do materials and practices in your class support students in successive grades? What resources are needed so that you and your colleagues may examine and discuss the progression of the standards?[8]

When we consider grade level at the onset of learning, we give all students—regardless of missing prerequisites—the opportunity to grapple with concepts appropriate for their age group. This is not to say that students missing prerequisites should not be taken into consideration as we design classroom learning; quite the opposite, we understand how complex and consuming meeting the needs of all learners can be. Just-in-time scaffolds—used to build on and respond to what students know to advance further learning—are one way to ensure that all students get exposure to grade-level work, while also accounting for unfinished learning. We also understand that remedial practices can be an appropriate tool in helping students develop skill sets and prerequisites that are essential for college and career success. But in thinking about scaffolding, there are a few questions we should consider: How might planning time be organized so that just-in-time scaffolds may be defined, chosen, practiced, and then discussed? How could you use such a process to determine whether or not the application of these scaffolds provides enough support for the students? Is there a climate of, and orientation toward, learning among grade-level teams and in the building at large, so that practitioners have the freedom to admit the areas of pedagogy they may need to grow and sharpen?

I have been talking about scaffolding as a critical part of engaging instruction, as teachers use it to ensure that every child gets frequent opportunities to read grade-level texts and engage in grade-level tasks. The scaffolding enhances learning and aids in the mastery of tasks. But I would like to be clear that scaffolding is more complex than simple modifications. Often we turn to instructional modifications as a first line of defense when students need support in a lesson. These modifications change the grade-level goals so that students can "stand on their own." However, instructional supports (or scaffolds) provide what each student needs to access the work *without* changing the grade-level goal.[9] By systematically building in multiple entry points as students are learning new skills, we preserve grade-level expectations and foster persistence. For instance, if in an eighth-grade class many students are struggling with disfluency as they read *To Kill a Mockingbird,* scaffolding and creating multiple entry points might mean incorporating read-alouds or audiobooks as students work their way through the text. When educators know the difference between a scaffold and a modification, and are adequately prepared to know when and where to apply the right support, then they are tending to the justice details in their teaching and prioritizing grade-level instruction.

If grade-level learning is an opportunity to energize students, it's clear that when students are placed in dismal learning environments, circling the drain of below grade-level skill, they become disengaged. When grade-level learning is absent, we often observe students like the young lady I encountered in the classroom in Louisiana. The response that is activated in the brain when learners face prolonged boredom[10] is no doubt one of the reasons that caused her to pull my arm and beg me—a complete stranger—to be her teacher.

Unfortunately the Louisana classroom that I mentioned in Chapter 2 wasn't the first time I was stopped by a student of color asking me to be their teacher while visiting a school. This child might have seen kinship in our braided hair; for other kids, sometimes it's just a feeling of familiarity that prompts them to speak up. Because of TNTP's 2018 report *The Opportunity Myth: What Students Can Show Us About How School Is Letting Them Down—and How to Fix It,* we know many students are plagued by boredom,[11] which is very much connected to a lack of grade-level instruction, and many rarely see an adult who looks like them in their schoolhouse. It's no wonder, then, that they hope if they make this appeal to me, someone will hear them.

The irony was that the school building in Louisiana had once been the site of a major event in the civil rights movement. When I visited some 50 years later, this student's experience clearly displayed that the fight for educational equity was far from over. Neither she nor her classmates were being educated to pursue liberty via grade-level instruction. I was convinced, even as the classroom teacher assured me this class had serious behavioral issues, even as the administration raved about the quality of education their students received as compared to *before* the realignment of school districting lines, and even as they pointed out that each student had access to their own laptop, that these students' civil rights were being violated; I was witnessing an educational malpractice occurring. A 30-minute observation like mine is, of course, just a snapshot in the life of a classroom. And yet, I know exactly what minutes and hours mean, in terms of learning lost, when students don't have access to grade-level work. One report found that students spend over 500 hours every school year on work that is not grade level.[12] Those hours add up when we talk about students' lack of access to grade-level work throughout their entire K–12 careers.

What barriers currently exist in your classroom or school that make it difficult to center grade-level instruction every day?

Engaging instruction is developing students' persistence in grade-level work that builds their interests. Engaging instruction ties that work to students' own knowledge and culture without disrupting their beliefs about who they are. Engaging students also means going beyond the edutainment strategies. As I mentioned before, this is the kind of classroom instruction that is meant to activate students' excitement, but that is often hollow in terms of deep engagement and fostering persistence with learning.

I'm guilty of employing edutainment more times in my classroom than I care to think about. I've used everything from treasure box incentives for students to math games, which were focused on rote memorization rather than supporting students in gaining the grade-level mathematical concepts. But engaging students can be more than flashy games and prizes; educators can also engage students by allowing them to move through productive struggle as learners. I inevitably learned as I grew as a practitioner that teaching is about more than getting students to do work in our classes; it is about expanding students' intellective capacity to further their learning not only in school but also for the rest of their lives as learners.

As I mentioned, as a middle school principal, I spent a significant amount of time focusing on teachers' beliefs about their students and, unfortunately, did not focus enough on expanding their teaching pedagogical toolkits. My teachers often complained about their students' lack of reading fluency when they wanted to read a grade-level book as a class. However, in retrospect, what I should have helped them understand was that students' fluency rate did not negate the students' intellectual ability to comprehend the text.

In addition to scaffolding, making equitable instruction the focus affords students opportunities to wrestle with new concepts, in contrast to being handed procedural approaches. Productive struggle means that we as educators promote persistence and creative problem-solving, and as a result, students gain a deeper understanding of more complex problems.

Too often in classrooms, we do not feel comfortable allowing our students to experience productive struggle or rigor, perhaps due to prerequisites they may be missing or unfinished learning the teacher must attend to. Before I had the pedagogical tools, I had to shift my mindset to embrace the scariest moment in my classroom: the moment when I had to teach something I hadn't learned myself, something I didn't have confidence or skill in. As I mentioned earlier, my mentor made it clear to me that I had to become okay with learning alongside my students. Creating a GLEAM classroom, especially one that fully engages our students, requires this particular kind of vulnerability. And for us to encourage that kind of brain-sweating that will engage young people's minds, we have to take on the same habits of mind we ask of our students.

Building engaging coursework also means redefining rigor. In education, just as engagement is not just about entertaining students, rigor is not about simply giving students more work, but about supporting them as they productively struggle in learning. In math, for example, we sometimes hand students the procedures, rather than allow students to productively wrestle with new concepts. Doing the latter helps to give meaning to *why* we use those procedures and how those procedures work in ways that are much more enduring. Productive struggle means that we, as educators, foster persistence but not to the point of frustration, and facilitate creative problem-solving. As a result, students gain a deeper understanding of more complex problems. When we encourage productive struggle, students develop understanding, and they progress in the learning process, but they may not always get the "right answer." This struggle, for both teachers and students, will take place at the intersection of both the grade-level standards and equitable instruction that are essential for closing the opportunity gap caused by systemic bias and racism.

What was a recent lesson or unit in your classroom that engaged your students in a productive struggle? Have you witnessed other educators engaging students in productive struggle in ways that could advance your own practice?

Affirming instruction means we honor and acknowledge students' ethnic, racial, cultural, and linguistic identities, and experiences, all within the context of grade-level work. Affirming instruction considers not only students' home and community lives, but also the experiences they've gained while developing their academic identities. This begins by considering what students already know, their cultural funds of knowledge, and their prior experiences that can support them in the task or text. At the core of affirming instruction is the deep belief that students do have cultural knowledge and experience from which to draw, that they are not blank slates, but rather young minds with cultural and personal understandings they bring into our classrooms every day. Affirming educators honor and acknowledge those understandings as tools to foster learning. By drawing authentic connections between academic concepts and topics and the knowledge students bring from their own communities, we place value on students' identities within the context of high-quality, grade-level work.

Teachers affirm young people when they intentionally identify occasions to value and develop students' identities as independent learners. Honoring and affirming students requires building relationships, knowing who your students are outside of the classroom, and being familiar with the communities in which they live. By encouraging the use of students' experiences, language, and culture during instruction, we value students' identities within the context of high-quality, grade-level work.

Affirming is also acknowledging and encouraging students' academic growth and specific needs as learners. Affirmation doesn't always come from achieving proficiency; it should also come from making mistakes and using failure as feedback. Professor and Harvard-trained psychologist Jeff Howard pleads with us[13] in the work of efficacy in education to use failure as an asset, especially in the classroom.

When I think about affirming classrooms and pedagogy, of course Mitchell always comes to mind. I have written a lot about the bias at work in his classroom, the colorblind lens, and the mindset-shifting teachers need to do. But I would love to paint a picture of what I imagine a supportive and affirming classroom could have looked like for Mitchell. In an affirming classroom, Mitchell and his classmates would *all* get to share the vocabulary of their home languages. Mitchell would be encouraged to use the cultural practice of call and response as a means to engage deeply with the storytelling. Instead of reprimanding him for call and response, his teacher might have paused and said, "Mitchell, I love how you are following along with me! I notice you're repeating. Where else do you do that kind of repeating?" Mitchell might have answered at home or at church and the teacher could have encouraged the class to repeat along with Mitchell, even if she herself was not familiar with the concept of call and response.

None of us have to be experts in each other's cultures to build affirming classrooms. We don't have to don cultural identities that are not our own, and we don't have to utilize music or words that don't resonate with us. Instead, to affirm students' cultural identities, we must listen to them, notice them, and be curious before attempting to punish their self-expression. Affirming classrooms provide spaces for *all* students to gain exposure to the cultural and linguistic practices of others. Perhaps most importantly, such classrooms allow students to use their own cultural and linguistic identities to build their academic identities. This means students, particularly students of color or those whose households do not reflect the dominant culture, do not have to divorce critical parts of themselves to be successful students.

So many of us are grappling with the question, how do we know if we're doing culturally affirming education? For me, the answer is a moment I had as a first-year teacher in Marietta, Georgia. My classroom was made up of about 50% Black students and 50% Latinx students. One day, a Latinx student raised his hand and asked about *chupacabras*. I had never heard the word before or the story, so I stopped the class and let him tell it. When he started talking, the classroom lit up; other students added their knowledge about *chupacabras*, what their parents and grandparents had told them about this monster. I went home that night, researched *chupacabras*, and reworked my lesson plans for the week. We spent *days* putting the *chupacabras* into every lesson: we wrote a story, the students drew what they thought a *chupacabra* looked like, and we incorporated the word into their phonemic awareness lessons. I asked students to think about what descriptive words they might use to talk about a scary *chupacabra* (teeth, fangs, and others). Together we affirmed students' stories and cultures, and we never moved away from rigor in our classroom or even the standards students were meant to learn. I had a blast and so did the students. For my part, as an educator, it didn't take a deep cultural knowledge to do this. It took only flexibility, humility, and the ability to release control to deliver affirming instruction.

Where in your classroom or school do you honor and center your students' ethnic, racial, and linguistic identities and experiences?

Finally, **Meaningful** instruction teaches students to understand and critique dominant cultural norms and to examine their community's social position to foster a sense of advocacy and change. By its very definition, meaningful instruction must be contextualized to the students, the time, and the place in which it is delivered. Teachers' meaningful activities and teaching tools are responsive to the conditions of students' lives, making the learning relevant to issues students may encounter in their everyday lives. Unfortunately, even our best curricula, frameworks, and guides cannot do the work of making lessons meaningful. What makes them meaningful is knowing and understanding the context in which you teach. Of course, this will change each year, depending on the students in your classroom. When real-world connections are made within the context of lessons, learners see the value in what is being taught, are more engaged, and even become co-creators in the learning process. Supporting students to understand and critique dominant cultural norms will foster a sense of advocacy and change. By critiquing dominant cultural norms and understanding our places within them, both teachers and students can challenge the call for assimilation and learn to assert our own values and perspectives.

One example of this comes from my experience at Marva Collins Preparatory School, which magnified the concept of "meaningful" for me. Later in my career, as my colleagues and I were developing GLEAM, I was grateful to be able to return to the memories of that experience. When I observed the combined second- and third-grade class as they moved through learning about *Animal Farm,* I watched their teacher skillfully weave in meaning at every turn. She aligned the antagonist and protagonist to real-life examples of civil rights leaders and injustices happening right in the students' neighborhood, including the fact that a large company was taking over the local playground to build another factory. She used this local fight to emphasize the concepts of organizing and resistance that grounded the book. The second and third graders related deeply and gave passionate and insightful responses that honestly, up until that point, I had never even imagined students their age could give. This teacher also helped students understand that the historical figures who were named in the book would be names they would hear many times in the future. In doing so, she was forming a piece of the scaffolds that other teachers would later build on. She supported students in building the skill of critique and applying it to their local context.

I now know that those Black and brown children at Marva Collins Preparatory School held a deep wisdom that came from being exposed to the outputs of systemic racism in their own neighborhoods. The events that led their parents to choose a Black-led, newly formed preparatory school, rather than the neighborhood school, also informed how they related to this content around injustice. I do not assume that all students of color are a monolith, but I do acknowledge that children of color—no matter how young—whose language, cultural context, and certainly local context are outside of the white dominant norm, hold a sociopolitical lens. It is essential that all children, especially children who have been the most marginalized, be given an opportunity to take their learning and make real-life connections that allow them to see the possibilities and the role their learning can play in making their communities, our nation, and our world a better place.

Meaningful instruction is one of the greatest assets we can give students of color, because it moves them from consumers to prosumers. Assimilation requires that children of color, children experiencing poverty, and children from other marginalized backgrounds be consumers of education to survive both school and the inequities in our broader society. Consumers buy a product and use it. However, prosumers are active in the creating, determining the viability of, and marketing a product. To make students of color prosumers means putting them in the driver's seat, not only of their education, but also in the sociopolitical contexts in which they live every day. Meaningful instruction empowers students and facilitates this shift.

Do students have opportunities in your classroom to examine their community's social position to foster a sense of advocacy and agency? If they don't now, what can you do—as soon as tomorrow—to ensure they do?

Reflecting on GLEAM

At its heart, GLEAM is about our mindsets as educators. We must recognize that in order to orient our classrooms and schools toward justice, we must do things differently and that requires both a strategy and a plan. GLEAM is meaningful only when it is coupled with our own mindset shifts, intention, and planning.

The beauty of GLEAM is that it rises above the political rhetoric of our time because all students—every last one of them—deserve a learning environment that is grade-level, engaging, affirming, and meaningful. All students flourish when their education not only acknowledges their identities but also the identities of others, affirming who they are as academics and as human beings. In our current education system, white students and students whose households are rooted in dominant culture get most of that affirmation in a very organic way. When we talk about GLEAM, we are talking about ensuring that all of our students have meaningful experiences. GLEAM is a means to push against what is not and to ensure justice *is* the reality.

I hope this examination of GLEAM provides a basis through which to view examples of GLEAM in action. I hope you use the case studies in the next chapter as a means of exploring the framework of GLEAM in your own practice. I want to reiterate the focus on mindsets so that GLEAM does not become yet another checklist in your work as an educator, but instead becomes the essence of who you are as an educator. GLEAM is not meant to make the pile of your work higher! It is meant to get you to stop and reconfigure how you do teaching and learning in your classroom and building.

6 GLEAM in Practice

Throughout this book, we have been laying the groundwork to understand the many legacies, layers, and lenses we educators must examine in order to shift our mindsets about what we need to do to deliver justice in our instruction. I've included the elements of GLEAM™ and how they work together to transform the educational experiences of our students, especially Black, Indigenous, and brown students, as well as those from low-income households.

I'm sure that as you've been reading this book you have been reflecting on your own educational experience and how students experience justice in the details of teaching and learning in both your room and the school more broadly. At UnboundEd we've been adjusting our frameworks and supporting teachers in implementing them in their classrooms for years now. In that time, we've had the opportunity to hear from thousands of teachers about their experiences in bringing GLEAM into their instruction. In this chapter, I will share some of those stories, and together we will look at what worked, what didn't, and how each of these scenarios may support your practice as you move toward GLEAM in your own school and classroom.

Most importantly, my aim is to provide you with the orientation and questions that will help you analyze your teaching and pedagogical practice along the continuum of GLEAM. I believe that once you are able to assess where you are on that continuum, you can begin to really utilize those questions to challenge and deepen your practice and more meaningfully align your school's and your classroom's practices, policies, and procedures toward justice.

You might get tired of hearing this, but it is important to remind you: there is no perfect checklist for grade-level, engaging, affirmative, and meaningful instruction. Instead, GLEAM is a consistent practice and a development of mindset and skill set. As educators, we will constantly need to recalibrate in our classrooms to push toward grade-level, engaging, affirming, and meaningful instruction. To achieve justice in the details of teaching and learning, we must embrace a continuous cycle of improvement, a process of Deconstruction, Reconstruction, and Construction[1] in our curricula and instruction. In so many ways, our adjusted version of Dr. Ladson-Billings' DRC—or Deconstruction, Reconstruction, and Construction—stands on the foundation of our five charges described in Chapter 3, and it emerged from our conversations about the "how" in achieving each element of GLEAM. When we as teachers and education leaders adopt GLEAM mindsets, we know that things need to change in our classrooms, but we don't always know how to achieve that change. DRC is the process that allows us to enact the GLEAM instruction we know students deserve.

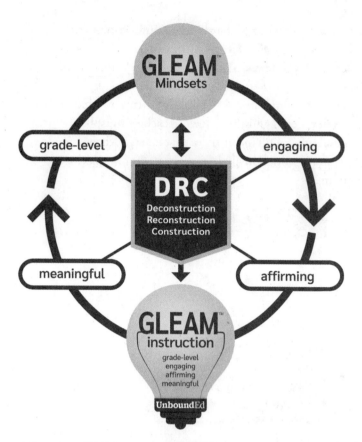

Adopting GLEAM mindsets begins our journey toward justice as educators, and Deconstruction, Reconstruction, Construction help us actualize GLEAM instruction in our classrooms.

Source: Springer Nature / CC BY 4.0.

Deconstruction, Reconstruction, and Construction

Once again, the work of Dr. Gloria Ladson-Billings helped my colleagues and me at UnboundEd to conceptualize Deconstruction, Reconstruction, and Construction. In "Yes, But How Do We Do It?," Dr. Ladson-Billings writes:

> *Deconstruction* refers to the ability to take apart the "official knowledge"[2] to expose its weaknesses, myths, distortions, and

omissions. *Construction* refers to the ability to build curriculum. Similar to the work that John Dewey[3] advocated, construction relies on experiences and knowledge that teachers and their students bring to the classroom. *Reconstruction* requires the work of rebuilding the curriculum that was previously taken apart and examined. It is never enough to tear down. Teachers must be prepared to build up and fill in the holes that emerge when students begin to use critical analysis as they attempt to make sense of the curriculum.[4]

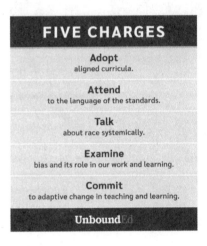

FIVE CHARGES

Adopt
aligned curricula.

Attend
to the language of the standards.

Talk
about race systemically.

Examine
bias and its role in our work and learning.

Commit
to adaptive change in teaching and learning.

UnboundEd

Deconstruction is the response to charges one and three: namely, "adopt aligned curriculum" and "talk about race systematically." But we also need to get concrete about what that means in practical terms. As educators, we have the responsibility and authority to deconstruct the curriculum to identify areas that may challenge our students' academic, racial, or cultural identities. When we deconstruct, we must annotate the existing curriculum to interrogate knowledge of the text, in order to assess if the units we are building are actually aligned with grade-level standards, and thus delivering a just educational experience. Additionally, deconstructing a curricular unit or lesson requires us to examine the possibility that biases undergird it and implicit systemic racism shapes it.

At UnboundEd, our understanding of Deconstruction, Reconstruction, and Construction is grounded in the work of Dr. Gloria Ladson-Billings. Our expansions and additions to her framework are visualized in this graphic.

Source: Springer Nature / CC BY 4.0.

Deconstruction can happen when we closely examine the illustrations or the underlying messages of a story or tackle the assumptions included in a particular task or set of materials. We can begin deconstruction by asking: What specific knowledge and skills are critical for students to meet the instructional objectives of the unit? Then, as you and your colleagues begin to talk about race systematically, you must ask, are students seeing only images of Indigenous communities in tribal garments for social and ceremonial occasions, or are there opportunities to showcase the continuance and creativity of Native American life and cultures?[5] Do the tasks or materials give underlying messages of "othering"—that is to say, is there an implicit message that further denotes one way of living while denouncing another?

DRC—Deconstruction, Reconstruction, Construction—really is a unit-level application of all elements of GLEAM, working through the five charges. Some critical questions that should guide you as you navigate Deconstruction are:

How does the unit scope and sequence build a coherent progression? This means establishing the criteria of success for unit mastery in your classroom and stripping away the curricular pieces that reinforce negative legacies and layers rather than supporting success.

How does the unit address unfinished instruction? This means determining if the existing or planned instructional supports will actually provide students with access to:

- The complexities identified in the central text;
- The concepts and ideas presented in the focus tasks; and
- The skills identified in the unit scope and sequence.

At its best, this question about unfinished learning helps you with what I mentioned in the previous chapter: to build scaffolding without sacrificing grade-level instruction.

Reconstruction means incorporating the experiences and knowledge that teachers and students bring to the classroom. This step is about co-constructing knowledge to adapt the existing curriculum and to rebuild the curriculum by filling in the holes you identified in the deconstruction process. Reconstruction aligns with charges two and five: to attend to the language of the standards and commit to adaptive change in our teaching and learning. Once we've done the work of deconstructing curriculum, only adaptive change will allow us to reimagine and rebuild it. To make the technical changes of Deconstruction and Reconstruction, there has to be an adaptive shift in our mindsets. Critical questions to consider as you reconstruct curricula are:

What resources can you use to enhance the curriculum and provide all students access to the grade-level content? How can you advance your pedagogical content knowledge and pedagogy to support engagement? You can develop your own set of texts or find materials and resources that address the list of informational topics you identified as critical knowledge in the central text, tasks, and materials of the unit. Even if you are in a district or a school where you can't introduce supplementary materials in this way, identifying these resources still helps you to advance your pedagogical content knowledge and skill.

Where in the scope and sequence of the unit can you leverage the key ideas and vocabulary that students will acquire from the additional resources you provide?

Or if you teach math, for example:

How can you launch math lessons leveraging your knowledge of across-grade coherence to connect mathematical ideas? You can create and use math warm-ups and instructional routines that ignite student thinking and offer multiple entry points based on the requisite skills for the lesson. Create a plan to incorporate information from the text, tasks, or materials you identified into daily instruction.

What funds of knowledge or experiences do students bring to this unit of study? How can the additional resources extend or affirm students' perspectives and lived experiences? Identify meaningful connection points between the deconstructed units of study, the complementary resources, and students' funds of knowledge. These connection points will help you strategically decide to incorporate meaningful cultural and social content into daily instruction. Incorporating students' funds of knowledge into daily instruction affirms their experiences and identities, while also building more meaningful units.

The first of our five charges, adopting an aligned curriculum, is a critical aspect of maintaining the bar for rigor and high expectations with integrity. For us, adopting an aligned curriculum is essential to achieving justice in the details of teaching and learning, and because of this we deviate slightly from Dr. Ladson-Billings on what construction means. In Dr. Ladson-Billings's framework, if the curriculum doesn't exist, you must build it. In ours, if your school district doesn't have it, you must find it and ensure that it aligns with the other grade-level standards of learning for your students.

By our definition, **Construction** requires us to apply the diversity of knowledge and experience in daily lessons to create meaningful learning experiences. Where Reconstruction helps map the arc or the story of the unit, one that illustrates the path to the learning outcome for students, Construction is where you take the arc of that unit and consider how it plays into a particular day or a specific lesson. This is a place to lean into meaning by weaving students' experiences into the story of the lesson, making it relevant to your students and intentionally connecting their home lives and school lives.

Construction occurs when teachers activate knowledge to implement the culturally relevant curriculum that has been revised during Reconstruction. This means incorporating the new and existing information from the text, tasks, or materials you identified during Reconstruction and then including them in daily instruction. You are highlighting the most important things necessary to refine a *new* curriculum or lesson plan, based on the original. In Construction, you are honing classroom learning experiences to attend to the cultural and social aspects of learning. The questions that guide construction are:

What aspects of the students' identities will be affirmed by this text/task? What aspects of the students' identities may be negatively impacted by this text? As you select the appropriate tasks and texts for this particular lesson, consider how you will mitigate negative cultural imagery and prioritize culturally affirming materials.

What specific information from the unit materials will you leverage in this lesson to support students' understanding of the central text and tasks? How will you adapt the content of this lesson to draw connections to students' identities and funds of knowledge? Once again, it's important to incorporate critical knowledge as well as students' own personal and experiential knowledge into daily instruction.

Where in this lesson will students have an opportunity to critique broader social inequities related to the world around them? What issues of power are represented in this text? How are people from historically, or actively marginalized, communities portrayed in this text? This is where you incorporate opportunities for your students to draw connections between the lesson and social inequalities within their local or global perspectives.

As we look into classrooms that are working to align themselves with GLEAM, I hope you will keep Deconstruction, Reconstruction, and Construction in mind. The guiding questions of DRC can help bring alive the concepts of "affirming" and "meaningful," and support you with questions that will guide your analysis of these classroom scenarios as well as influence your unit and lesson level planning.

Let's get concrete. If you have time, read each of these scenarios twice. The first time, see what you notice and pay attention to what aspects of GLEAM stand out to you. After that first reading, sit down with a colleague or jot notes down yourself about where you saw grade-level, engaging, affirming, and meaningful instruction take place. On the second read-through, look at our "Seeing GLEAM" section after each scenario and compare your own observations to ours. Reflect on the changes you can make immediately in your own lessons to push instruction further along the GLEAM continuum.

Ms. Arberg's Story (GLEAM in Math)

For many educators, operationalizing GLEAM in English language or humanities classrooms seems more straightforward and aligned with the content, but when it comes to math and the sciences, we tend to be less practiced in how to think about cultural relevance and how to build identity-affirming lesson plans. But understanding the vast racial disparities that exist for young people in science and math from kindergarten through their careers, focusing on the fact that *justice is found in the details of teaching and learning*[8] becomes just as critical, maybe even more so, in these subjects.

UnboundEd's Director of Mathematics Leadership, Jen Arberg, has a simple and incredible example I love to share when talking to educators about how to overcome their hesitation around GLEAM in mathematics. Ms. Arberg was teaching a community group of 25 adults from faith groups and parent support groups. They were not educators. The group met monthly on different topics, and this month they wanted to learn and understand more about culturally relevant instruction. To get a sense of the crowd, Ms. Arberg had attended their Zoom meetings in the months leading up to her presentation, and for the most part cameras were off, and people were not engaging with the speakers or content.

To help this group of community members understand what culturally relevant instruction could look like in practice, Ms. Arberg decided to teach them based on a seventh-grade math lesson that introduced proportional relationships with tables. The goals[6] of the lesson, according to the lesson plan Ms. Arberg used, were to ensure that students—in this case the adult learners—could:

- Comprehend that the phrase "proportional relationship" (in spoken and written language) refers to when two quantities are related by multiplying by a "constant of proportionality."

- Describe (orally and in writing) relationships between rows or between columns in a table that represent a proportional relationship.

- Explain (orally) how to calculate missing values in a table that represents a proportional relationship.

Ms. Arberg began by defining the concept of proportions and giving the community members the lesson goals. To provide a real-world example of proportions, Ms. Arberg explained that a woman wants to make six cups of rice for a dinner party of 10–12 guests.

After setting up the scenario, Ms. Arberg paused and asked, "Who here has made rice? Based on your experience, does that sound like a reasonable amount of rice?" At this moment, the participants turned on their cameras, came off of mute, and began to share a little of their own personal experiences around cooking rice. Ms. Arberg continued, "And how do you make your rice?" People were sharing family recipes, their cultural standards for rice cooking, the spices they used in their rice, and even how much rice they felt was appropriate to cook per person. Some used the finger test when cooking their rice, some washed their rice before cooking, some preferred their rice a little more al dente, and others liked theirs more mushy. Ms. Arberg's straightforward question about rice soon became a conversation that highlighted cultural contexts of traditions, language, and customs around preparation and consumption. There was even a small debate about whether six cups of rice was the right amount for this fictitious dinner party of 10 to12. Ms. Arberg would facilitate all of this to take the group back to the student-facing task outlined in the lesson plan: determining how many cups of rice would serve 10 people.

Throughout the conversation, Ms. Arberg brought people's cultural contexts around rice into this lesson about proportions, and she drove them back to the lesson's goals. Ms. Arberg launched the math task, using illustrative math as well as the seventh-grade math standards. She had the participants break out into groups where they did visual representations of the proportions problem; groups made tables and charts, and Ms. Arberg created a Google jamboard where they could all see their work captured. She then asked the whole group what connections they saw between each visual representation, both concrete and abstract. Ms. Arberg's focus was not on the answers, but rather on the strategies participants used to arrive at an understanding of proportions. After the lesson, Ms. Arberg was able to debrief with her participants about what it meant to affirm their mathematical identities by incorporating their cultural contexts.

Before you read on, either on your own or with a colleague, ask:

What elements of GLEAM™ (Grade-Level, Engaging, Affirming, and Meaningful) instructions were present in this lesson?

Seeing GLEAM in Ms. Arberg's Rice Lesson

I want to pause here and acknowledge the tension that often arises when I talk to educators about GLEAM in math. There is such national urgency around improving our K–12 students' math scores that sometimes I hear pushback to the tune of, "I barely have time to cover all the required concepts and skills in a year, I don't have time to talk about rice." I have also felt this all-consuming urgency at various times in my career, and I have sacrificed meaning and engagement in order to drill concepts and skills. But even if you are able to dismiss the racial and social justice benefits of bringing GLEAM into math instruction, it's impossible to dismiss the cognitive benefits of using schema[7] and scaffolding to enhance memory and learning. Affirming content and experiential knowledge are the work of teaching, and when we allow students to bring their emotional and personal experiences into the classroom, math stops being a chore they must endure, and becomes a technical skill that is integral to their lives. It is critical then that as educators—especially those who are in science, technology, engineering, and math fields—that we prioritize a mindset shift, from seeing students' preexisting knowledge, experiences, and cultures as classroom distractions, to seeing them as a positive means to improve cognition, processing, and retention.

When I asked Ms. Arberg about including this story, she protested, saying this was just a basic example of GLEAM pedagogy, but I think that when we talk about what GLEAM is in areas like science and math, the simplicity of this lesson plan is its strength. Of course, Ms. Arberg's participants were not students, but her goal in using the Open-Up 7.2.2. lesson plan was to illustrate that culturally affirming pedagogy could be easily implemented within grade-level standards.

Ms. Arberg engaged her participants' funds of knowledge by asking them about their own experiences with cooking and preparing rice for large groups. This offered an opportunity for the participants to engage in discussion and problem-solving that could be then used in service of the math learning objectives, which was one important step in moving this lesson along the GLEAM continuum. Additionally, Ms. Arberg affirmed students' funds of knowledge and their linguistic diversity, as well as their cultural identities by grounding the lesson in their understanding of how to make rice in their own homes as well as their own cultures.

Admittedly, Ms. Arberg's lesson does not address the meaningful aspect of GLEAM, because it falls short on addressing local or community-based issues and topics related to the goals of the lesson. Nor does it help students apply the principles to the real world in ways that connect to students' lived experiences, nor does it embody anti-racism. Ms. Arberg could have taken the time to elicit a conversation about where the earliest archaeological evidence about rice comes from (central and eastern China) and how rice became a global grain that in some populations is the most significant source of nutrition. However, even just achieving the GLEAM aspect of the framework is a basis upon which to build toward meaningful instruction in the future.

In what ways do you think a similar lesson on proportions could embody anti-racism or challenge inequality?

Ms. Carvajal's Story (GLEAM in ELA)

One of UnboundEd's seasoned facilitators, Hannah Turner, shared this story. Ms. Turner supports our National Institute and is a seventh-grade administrator at a middle school in Maryland. She is a part of the English Language Development (ELD) team, which includes Ms. Carvajal, Mr. Neto, Ms. Turner, Ms. Bonig, and Ms. Parrish. This team provides ELA instruction to a cohort of multilingual learners who span the sixth, seventh, and eighth grades. In this cohort, the English Language Development Levels are 2 through 4.4, according to the ELD scale used by WIDA, a resource for educators that assesses English language proficiency. On the WIDA scale, students' English proficiency ranges from the ability to "understand how precise meanings are created through everyday, cross-disciplinary, and technical language through a growing number of words and phrases in a variety of contexts" (Level 2) to the ability to understand the same dynamics "through a variety of words and phrases such as adverbials of time, manner, and place; verb types; and abstract nouns" (Level 6).[8]

In light of the Covid-19 pandemic students and teachers were experiencing at the time of this story, this cohort of multilingual students in Maryland had been using recently updated materials about the history of epidemics. The particular resources they used came from the school's seventh-grade curriculum and were being used as a framework for all grade-level English Language Development classes. While in other years the ELD team would have used a sixth-grade curriculum for sixth-grade students, a seventh-grade curriculum for seventh-grade students, and so forth, the team instead decided to begin with the same curriculum across the sixth to eighth grades to increase the degree of collaboration that otherwise would not be possible; this felt necessary in a school year of so many unprecedented challenges.

The topic of epidemics was both timely and relevant for students. The Expeditionary Learning guidance[9] that the ELD team used urged teachers to exercise caution with the epidemic unit because it was developed pre-COVID and was now a sensitive topic. As a result, the ELD team assigned a task to students in the first week of school in which they interviewed their caregivers in their home language and asked for their caregiver's thoughts on the teaching of this unit. Overall, across grade levels and ELD levels, caregivers agreed with educators that the unit would be timely and important.

As students developed their understanding of medical epidemics, they began to take note of things they heard outside of the classroom about epidemics that did not precisely fit the definition that their ELD teachers had provided in class or the definition in their anchor text, *Patient Zero*[10]—a book that focuses on a different medical epidemic throughout history in each chapter. As the unit unfolded, students occasionally broached and named the subject of the "racism epidemic" they had heard about on social media or their parents talked about after watching the news.

The ELD team convened regularly throughout the unit for collaborative planning and examined the Guiding Questions and Big

Ideas of the Expeditionary Learning Unit[11] on epidemics.
They included:

I. What are epidemics? How do they develop?

- Epidemics can be medical or social. There are similarities and
differences to epidemics, depending on whether they are social
or medical in nature.

- Social epidemics can be positive or negative.

- Epidemics spread through contagion as well as
social networks.

II. How do people respond to an epidemic?

- People's response to epidemics affects their overall impact.
Epidemics can be contained when people respond with
positive character traits and logic.

- When people respond with fear and selfishness, epidemics
often spread.

III. What is the role of character and mindset in solving
epidemic crises?

- Epidemiologists can respond to epidemics with integrity,
initiative, responsibility, and perseverance. Doctors or
caregivers can respond to patients with compassion, respect,
and empathy.

IV. What methods and tools help people to solve epidemics?

- People use logic, the scientific method, and innovation to
solve mysterious epidemics.

Throughout this process, the team discussed an opportunity to
pivot to social epidemics, specifically racism, while maintaining the
integrity of the guiding questions and the assessed standards of the
unit as well as to address student questions. Ms. Turner, who was a
part of the ELD team, had been an UnboundEd facilitator, an

experience that had encouraged her to shift her own personal lenses and provided her with the skill set to support the team in evolving the lesson around epidemics. The ELD team designed a unit within the larger epidemics unit and utilized the same framework that they saw with Expeditionary Learning. They used Jason Reynolds' and Ibram X. Kendi's young adult text, *Stamped: Racism, Antiracism, and You,* to orient students to the history of racism in the same way that *Patient Zero* oriented students to the history of epidemics.

Students were asked to bring their current understanding of race and racism into the classroom, but students acknowledged they did not understand much of what they had encountered. Many students in the cohort were newcomers to the United States and admitted that their perception of the United States was based mainly upon the ideal of a nation where everyone was free and equal. They weren't sure how to contend with what they had always believed about the United States and what they were now hearing. Other students in the class who had lived in the United States for their whole lives agreed they were curious and concerned about the topic.

As students engaged with the text and the guiding questions, they began to express interest in taking some sort of action step. On social media, they saw influencers had taken action by donating money or protesting, but as middle school students they recognized that their means to participate in those ways were often not feasible or lasting. The English Language Development teachers were excited, then, to reveal their idea for a culminating project. This school district in Maryland had begun conducting an anti-racist audit during the time in which students were learning about epidemics. The ELD team was aware that the district's Board of Education was soliciting student and community voices from around the state concerning the district's anti-racist work, and the team believed that this was an opportunity for students to engage with an authentic task.

The ELD teachers told students that in many ways the lesson was serendipitous. Thanks to students' own curiosity and the teachers' knowledge of Kendi's and Reynolds' work, the class was able to engage in this meaningful study as a supplement to the original lesson. However, perhaps engaging in something larger, more permanent, and county-wide could expand the learning even further. The teachers shared that students would be writing a persuasive letter to their Board of Education. The letter would be a call to action to systemize the teaching of the history of race within American history, and the letters would align to writing anchor standards, with specific grade levels and language development levels appropriately supported in the different classes.

Let's pause here and consider:

What reflections do you have on the DRC—Deconstruction, Reconstruction, Construction—and GLEAM frameworks as you consider Ms. Carvajal and the English Language Development team's lesson on epidemics? What was helpful to read? What ideas or strategies challenged you?

Seeing GLEAM in Ms. Carvajal's Epidemic Lesson

Before we get to the GLEAM of Ms. Carvajal's and the ELD team's lesson on epidemics, I want to pause and acknowledge the work of Deconstruction, Reconstruction, and Construction that the team took in reimagining their lesson plans. *Deconstruction* began when the ELD team first decided to overhaul the epidemics lesson to increase collaboration across their sixth- to eighth-grade classrooms and to address the biases that may have existed in the framework of the original curricula.[12] *Reconstruction* came as they included the current context of COVID-19 as well as the social and racial epidemics, which had been the focus of protests in 2020. The ELD team's

Reconstruction process also included soliciting the voices and input of students' caregivers. Finally, *Construction* was the execution of the revised lesson, their iteration throughout the lesson's implementation, and most important, inclusion of student voices as they did so.

As we look through a GLEAM lens, we see initially that the teaching team did offer grade-level instruction (and above) to the sixth- and seventh-grade students. However, the eighth-grade students in ELD did not receive grade-level instruction since the team chose to use seventh-grade standards. It's important to note that GLEAM exists on a continuum. We understand that as you aim for GLEAM you might also land at a decision like this. But it's important that even as you focus on a seventh-grade text in a lesson like Ms. Carvajal's, you are also thoughtful and intentional about places in the lesson where eighth-grade students are exposed to eighth-grade standards and learning around that text. We should also note that the ELD team was careful around the decisions to dip into a seventh-grade text with the intention of hitting the eighth-grade-level standards, following up to ensure that while a younger text was used, students did not *stay* below grade level.

This lesson's rigorous topic provided a great example of engaging, as the unit undoubtedly included new scientific and medical terminology. Students were challenged not only to learn the definitions of these new words, but also to deepen their understanding by observing how those terms were used in contexts outside of the classroom. Here, Ms. Carvajal and her team explicitly taught cognitive routines and fostered academic discussion and problem solving. Additionally, the timeliness of the topic (a factor that was thoughtfully deconstructed, reconstructed, and constructed by the ELD team) drew on students' funds of knowledge and increased students' deep engagement with the lesson.

The ELD team identified an opportunity to affirm students by addressing the questions they had about social epidemics, specifically racism. The team affirmed students' funds of knowledge around the racial unrest and protests they had observed over the past few years, pushing their lesson further along on the GLEAM continuum. Perhaps a meaningful aspect of the lesson could have been deepened by allowing students to co-create more options in the form and structure of the final assignment. However, the intention with which Ms. Carvajal and the ELD team planned their lesson to meet their students' and their families' needs is at the heart of how to craft meaningful instruction. By acknowledging that epidemics are also things that plague this community of students, they addressed local and community-based issues and made meaningful connections to the real world. It is important to note that Ms. Carvajal's students were living just outside of Washington, DC, during the uprisings in the summer of 2020; including the racial unrest in this lesson attended to students' specific cultural and social context in a meaningful way. Of course, sociopolitical consciousness is often hard to illustrate, and the issues relevant to students may change or be different, but being intentional during unit planning is necessary to be successful with planning for the M—meaning—in GLEAM.

We know that the political realities of your school or school district may differ from that of Ms. Carvajal and the ELD team. At our UnboundEd Standards Institutes, we have heard educators share their challenges with implementing critical and rigorous pedagogy. At this polarized time in education, it might seem like asking parents is an easy way to have your curriculum ruled too controversial or offensive. However, the ELD's decision to interview caregivers about the upcoming lesson was a thoughtful way to not only keep families informed, but also to *increase* buy-in on what could have been perceived, on its surface, as a controversial topic. Overwhelmingly, the caregivers saw the lesson as valuable and timely, and engaging parent feedback turned out to be a tool for consensus building. I can't promise you a strategy like this will always work, but it is a pertinent cooperative move that you can use to explain the grade-level learning and intention behind the lesson.

Mr. Bowman's Story (GLEAM in Science)

The seventh-grade science unit on genetics has always been a favorite for Mr. Bowman. This year, as usual, the unit began with students exploring disorders that are passed down genetically in human beings. Students watched a CNN video highlighting a family's five-year-old daughter who had a neurological genetic disorder—an introduction that prompted many questions among students. Students in Mr. Bowman's class also read a Request for Report that provided an introductory glimpse of four genetic disorders that students would soon research. A Request for Report is a document—also used by professional scientists—that describes the scope of the project, provides important background information, and defines the criteria and constraints of the project.

Mr. Bowman provided a link for students to post questions that arose as they navigated the reading, and he also encouraged students to use a close reading strategy that included:

- Circling unknown vocabulary words
- Using exclamation points for concepts students want to learn more about
- Utilizing check marks for concepts in which students have some background knowledge or familiarity
- Generating questions in the margins

In past years, the unit has generated a lot of excitement, and students this year began to share their own genetic traits and ask questions about themselves and their families. One student asked, "My uncle has sickle cell anemia, but my mom doesn't and he's her brother. Why did it skip her?" Another wondered, "My neighbor's dog has one blue eye and the other eye is light brown. How does she have different colored eyes? Can humans have different colored eyes?" Students learned more about four key genetic disorders, and they were interested to discover that while sickle cell and cystic fibrosis disorders could affect anyone, there is a higher rate of incidence among specific groups of people.

This was a big unit that covered a range of foundational scientific concepts. Mr. Bowman emphasized the importance of vocabulary in this unit, but assured students they would be given many opportunities to experience and apply vocabulary in the lead up to their culminating project. He offered students a choice in selecting one of the four genetic disorders as well as options for customizing the ways they displayed their information. Students' interest varied as they moved through the research. For the most part, readers who were on or above grade level were more independently successful at finding and organizing the required information. Meanwhile, below-grade-level readers, especially the ELL and special education students in Mr. Bowman's class, required more differentiated support with navigating the various resources and organizing the information.

Mr. Bowman was fortunate to have a para-educator who spoke Spanish. Her presence ensured that the class was able to support students with limited English proficiency. But even with that additional help, balancing task-completion rates and the needs of specific students was a challenge. Mr. Bowman offered additional online learning resources for students to explore. The Request for Report asked students to take on the role of a genetic counselor and to counsel prospective parents on the possible outcomes and management options for having children with a genetic disorder.

One of the most challenging lessons within this unit centered on students using Punnett squares as models to predict outcomes for their prospective parents and counsel them on the details and probability of passing on a genetic disorder. Mastering Punnett squares was critical in expanding students' recognition of patterns and cause-and-effect relationships, which of course, is a foundational skill in the sciences and across disciplines. Several students struggled with the math application required for Punnett squares and needed more one-on-one review—of fractions and percentages—to successfully predict outcomes.

In one section of the unit, students worked in table groups and attempted to sort a variety of traits as either something they received biologically from their parents, like their height, or something they gained on their own, like learning to ride a bike. In addition, the group needed to develop a definition for these acquired versus inherited traits. Interestingly, many groups positioned traits like being good at a sport or playing a musical instrument in the middle between acquired and inherited.

One student, Mackenzie, argued, "I am good at basketball like my dad."

Mr. Bowman encouraged Mackenzie to analyze this trait a little deeper. "What makes you good at basketball?"

Mackenzie replied, "I practice every day."

"Is practicing inherited from your parents?"

Mackenzie thought about it and decided, "No, but I am tall like my dad, and my doctor says that I am supposed to grow to almost 6 feet."

Mr. Bowman pushed her further, "Okay, what determines how tall we will become?"

Mackenzie concluded, "The genes that we have in our DNA. We get that from our parents. My mom is not tall, so I must get that from my dad. I understand . . . the trait for being taller gives me an advantage and helps me be better at basketball, but practicing is something I control and also helps me be better."

Questions like these laid the groundwork for students to make connections to new, academic vocabulary: words and phrases like "dominant and recessive traits," "heterozygous" and "homozygous," and "genotypes." And as a final learning experience—to tie in all of the complex pieces of this massive unit—Mr. Bowman implemented a virtual simulation allowing students to conduct breeding experiments on mice.

Let's pause briefly.

What thoughts on the Deconstruction, Reconstruction, and Construction process came up for you as you read about Mr. Bowman's lesson? What elements of GLEAM were most evident in the lesson design?

GLEAM in Mr. Bowman's Genetics Lesson

Once again, I chose Mr. Bowman's story to highlight that while implementing GLEAM in science, technology, engineering, and math classrooms might sound daunting, it doesn't have to be. Mr. Bowman's lesson drew directly from his state's seventh-grade standards and focuses on three-dimensional science learning, as outlined by the framework of the National Research Council (NRC). In this three-dimensional learning model, students use science and engineering practices and crosscutting—concepts applicable across scientific domains—to help make sense of disciplinary core ideas.[13] In science, it is critical for students to use the practices of asking questions and using models; these skills begin to reveal predictable patterns and cause-and-effect relationships in the outcomes. Mr. Bowman and his colleagues on the science team ensured that the lesson fell directly within the grade-level standards. Importantly, he made accommodations for ELL students that ensured students had the linguistic scaffolding they needed to access the grade-level curriculum.

From the beginning of this lesson on genetics, Mr. Bowman engaged students by using their funds of knowledge to establish a difference between acquired and inherited traits and, later, to support students' understanding of how parental genotypes affect the possible outcomes for offspring based on the dominant and recessive alleles they carried. Engagement in Mr. Bowman's class also included providing linguistic scaffolding that allowed students to engage with productive struggle as they navigated through the multi-faceted lesson on genetics. Punnett squares and other subunits explicitly taught cognitive routines that would serve them in future scientific lessons.

Mr. Bowman affirmed students through collective learning as well as being responsive to students' funds of knowledge about their own personal and familial genetics. However, meaningful instruction for this lesson could definitely have been bolstered by tying the learning about genetics to topics or issues in students' local or community-based contexts. For instance, students could reflect on how pollutants in the drinking water of their city might create genetic mutations or how food deserts and lack of healthy food access could impact the genetics of families living in the same area for generations. And while the lesson most assuredly was applicable to students' real-world experiences, the lesson did not embody anti-racism or challenge inequity with relation to the topic.

When we consider the Deconstruction, Reconstruction, Construction framework, there were more opportunities for Mr. Bowman and the seventh-grade science teaching team to implement DRC in this lesson design. Perhaps they could have brought in texts or materials that discussed racial disparities in the historic study and dissemination of information on genetics. Maybe they could have incorporated materials that allowed students the opportunity to connect the study of genetics to false claims made throughout history about societal constructs like race and intelligence. Of course, these are not the only ways to Reconstruct or Construct this particular lesson, but they could have been a starting point for meaningful disruption.

Overall, Mr. Bowman's story helps us understand how a science lesson might exist (and might be furthered) on the continuum that is GLEAM.

Looking through a GLEAM Lens

As a framework, GLEAM allows us to see the possibilities that exist in the lessons we create. It also helps us unearth the mindsets, both within ourselves and the system, that limit our lessons and create barriers, rather than entry points, for students. Because GLEAM is not a checklist, sometimes your lessons will lean heavily into affirming, more than any other aspect of GLEAM. At other times, it might be critical to focus on providing the right scaffold to engage students in productive struggle. Again, GLEAM is a way to reframe how we think about curriculum and lesson design.

As educators, we have the responsibility to deconstruct lessons that no longer serve our students, to reconstruct these lessons in ways that fill up the holes that originally made those lessons untenable, and finally to construct a new lesson that affirms student identity, aligns with their grade-level standards, and encourages them to challenge the status quo. It is a lofty goal, but one that is achievable at the unit, curricular, and school levels if we dare to center justice in the details of teaching and learning.

7 Our Equity Charge

Even though our challenges are many, I still get excited when I am talking to new or aspiring teachers. I try to communicate that they are entering a group of special folks, and to remind them that collectively we are a community that has shifted and can shift our nation's trajectory to the creeds it was built upon. But most importantly, I try to emphasize that as a community, we, the teachers and the educators of this world, influence everyone.

I know that in my own journey I've had many naysayers. As a teacher, I've had school leaders who did not believe my children should be exposed to comprehensive, affirming, research-based literacy instruction. As a principal, I have had teachers who were nervous or intimidated by new ideas or ways of thinking. I've had school districts and administrations design restrictive policies that incentivized me to create schools that functioned more as carceral centers than as places for joyful exploration and curious discovery. Over and over again, I have encountered stakeholders who believed the least of my students and, honestly, of me. Throughout all of that, perhaps one of the toughest voices to overcome was my own: the voice that told me to stay safely in the realm of the status quo and not rock the boat, the one who heard the resistance from school leaders and retreated into the steadier ground of assimilation, and the one who told me that the work of delivering true justice and equity was a little too hard at that moment or was useless to pursue because it is just the way things are.

However, in those same conversations with new and upcoming teachers, I stress that as educators, as people who have chosen this path, we are really on a hero's journey. It is a powerful assignment to stand in front of folks and to ignite the want and the need to learn something. For many of us, teaching begins as a calling. But like all heroes' journeys, even as you encounter naysayers along your path, you will also encounter mentors and supporters who will help make the road a little easier and the path that much clearer. No matter what, even in your own pursuit of learning as a professional and person, you can't lose sight of the goal. I hope this book will be one of the touchstones on your path, a small light that will help you keep that fire burning in your belly. Because you've chosen a marvelous road, a road that ensures justice for every single student that you encounter on your path in the future.

In almost every chapter of this book, you've heard me talk about the importance of mindset shifts as we attend to the work of justice in the details of teaching and learning. I am sure the idea of this type of transformation—one that is both so deeply personal and at once inextricably tied to centuries of legacies, layers, and lenses—can seem herculean, maybe even impossible, but I want to assure you there is nothing more possible and more critical to your teaching. But unlike the hero's journeys of mythical figures like Hercules, you are not alone. You stand as one in a mighty community of millions. No matter when in your walk as an educator you've come to this question of justice and equity, you have arrived at the right moment, and this community, our UnboundEd Edusphere, is ready to welcome you.

Remembering Our Why

At UnboundEd our vision is a world in which educators actively work together to dismantle systemic racism by providing grade-level, engaging, affirming, and meaningful instruction. Collectively, we are focused on justice in the details of teaching and learning to eliminate the predictability of educational outcomes by race. This is our rallying cry and our North Star. This is the fire that fuels us even when we are inevitably daunted in the work of progress. By embracing GLEAM™, we are acknowledging that teaching is an art, science, and a craft, but it is also a tool for equity and a powerful engine for societal change. In order for us to meet the possibilities of our calling, it is critical that we always remember why justice is necessary in the first place.

In 2021, Dr. Francesca López and a research team at the Aspen Institute authored a brief titled, *United We Learn: Honoring America's Racial and Ethnic Diversity in Education*.[1] This two-page text analyzed a wide range of research across K–12 educational systems and found what we know to be true: that both race and racial inequity color children's educational experience at nearly every age and grade level. According to Dr. Lopez, "A recent Children and Racism study commissioned by Sesame Workshop with children ages 6–11 and their parents, found 86% of children think people in the US are treated unfairly based on race. Nearly half the children surveyed reported that racism was top of mind, with reports of racism more prevalent in responses of Black children."[2] Instead of ignoring these accounts from students, the brief encourages educators not only to affirm students' cultural and academic identities and actively work to create a sense of belonging in the classroom, but also to lean into conversations about race and racism. "Research shows discussing race and racism in school reduces prejudice among White students and students of color."[3]

When I read Dr. López's report, it affirmed so many things about not only our approach to GLEAM, but why grade-level, engaging, affirming, and meaningful instruction is so critical. The GLEAM hypothesis is that only when mindset and planning are purposefully put into the service of grade-level, engaging, affirming, and meaningful instruction do we see the kinds of teacher actions and student experiences that exemplify culturally relevant teaching, or what we hope becomes the standard for just good teaching. We've focused on what planning looks like, what the elements of GLEAM are in practice, and what teachers must shift in their own thinking to accomplish the goal of justice in the details of teaching and learning. Now I want us to zero in on the student experience. Because no matter how entrenched racism is in every aspect of our society, and no matter how pervasive the legacies of power and disenfranchisement are, *we* are fully capable of changing the student experience, one classroom, one school, or one school district at a time.

It is absolutely crucial that we focus on what can be done when we center the brilliance and possibility of our Black, Indigenous, and brown students at every stage of their educational development. A good friend of mine, Lydia Ramos-Mendoza, puts it this way: no matter how grim our graduation numbers, test scores, or other outcomes, we would never on the first day of kindergarten tell parents and caregivers they should just give up. It would be inconceivable that we would inform families as they walk up to the school, bright eyed and hopeful, on that first day that because 30% of students will not graduate they should just turn around and go home. As educators, as people who want to see children and young people flourish, we would never want to quell hope in this way.

And yet, the data shows us that is just what's happening every day in schools around the country. We've discussed the fact that Black preschoolers are more likely to be suspended than their white counterparts.[4] In terms of student experience, this means three- and four-year-olds are facing disciplinary measures that alienate them both from their learning and from their peers. But equally alarming is the fact that these tiny Black children face more ongoing and negative scrutiny from teachers than white children[5] and are more likely to face complaints about their behavior, a stigma that can have negative implications on their elementary school academic performance.[6] Mitchell's experience—having a teacher silence him while he was trying to participate in story time—compounds the stigma and makes him less likely to speak up, to share new ideas, and to fully engage in future classrooms, ultimately dimming his light for learning.

Tracking and racial bias in course enrollment means that even when they attend schools that offer advanced course work, many students of color are shut out of those opportunities. According to The Education Trust, "Black students are 14% of eighth graders in schools that offer eighth grade Algebra I, but only 10% of students enrolled in the course. Similarly, Latino students are 24% of eighth graders in schools with eighth grade Algebra I, but they comprise only 18% of eighth grade Algebra I enrollment."[7] At the high school level this means Black, Indigenous, and Latinx students have less access to the honors, Advanced Placement (AP), and International Baccalaureate (IB) courses that have become a critical consideration in college admissions. The Education Trust calculates: "If Black and Latino students had a fair chance to enroll, we would see 157,513 more Black students and 68,102 more Latino students in AP courses."[8] This, coupled with a well-documented and racially informed discipline gap,[9] means that throughout their K–12 educational careers, Black, Indigenous, and brown students are faced with teachers who are more likely to scrutinize for chances to discipline them rather than promote them. In the end, the opportunity to display, hone, and expand their brilliance is offered only in scant proportions to the students of color who comprise the majority of our K–12 public school population.

At multiple points throughout their educational tenures—and through absolutely no fault of their own—our system grinds down hope in Black, Indigenous, and brown children, as well as children from low-income households. And if we allow it, the system will also grind down the hope in our vision of their success. Knowing all of this, it is critical we make hope both the antidote and one of the key strategies in our arsenal of teaching skills.

The Formula of Hope

The truth is that we are all sitting in the paralyzing awareness of decades, even centuries, of unjust policies, practices, and procedures. It is impossible, maybe even inhumane, to leave that reality unacknowledged. As a nation, America squirms away from the implications of what these histories and their legacies mean in the modern day. Because sometimes, looking these entrenched injustices in the face feels like an unraveling, an undoing.

It is exhausting to contemplate the generations of cruelty and harm that led to my own education and the educational reality our students face today. I am more than a little weary. Add a crushing pandemic, increasingly more restrictive laws, banned books and censorship, and a persistent undervaluing of our profession, I know you are weary, too. When facing this type of weariness, anger, and trauma, hope might seem like a flimsy defense. But I've found that one of the only ways to counter weariness is to ignite hope.

According to Brené Brown, hope means having a plan for where you're going.[10] Hope is knowing what you are aiming for. Hope is giving yourself the permission and grace to change pathways and shift lanes when the thing that you're doing isn't working, because you still have your eyes on the prize. Hope is more than naïve optimism. Hope is a powerful antidote to the poisons of our time.

Once, on a phone call with the incredible Dr. Lisa Delpit, a colleague and I were discussing a project on which we were hoping she would advise us. Dr. Delpit paused us mid-conversation and told us that throughout her career she also felt like the ideas and strategies she developed would put a definitive end to the predictability of educational outcomes by race. But she wanted us to understand that in our lifetime, "You are not extinguishing it, but are taking us further down the path for future generations." Dr. Delpit wasn't doom-and-glooming us, but telling us why we should hold on. The kind of justice we seek—for ourselves and for our students—is not going to happen in a single catch phrase or a new set of curriculum materials, but it will come through the culmination of all of this work throughout time. Dr. Delpit reminds us of what Dr. King foretold, that "the arc of the moral universe is long, but it bends toward justice." Change takes a long time, but it does happen.

Part of the source of our collective weariness is the hope that one day we'll wake up and, immediately, racism will be gone. The kind of rugged hope we need to finish our leg of the journey is derived from clarity both about the destination and distance our own feet can carry us along the path. And when we cultivate hope as a practice within ourselves, we are better positioned to elicit that same hope in our students.

In the Bible and the Talmud, Joseph—whose 11 brothers were so jealous of him that they sold him into slavery—had his relatives promise that his bones would be buried in the land that was promised to his ancestors. When the exodus finally happened, his relatives carried his bones to the Promised Land. Joseph knew that just because he wasn't going to see the end of the journey, he should never stop pursuing it, because he had a critical part to play. Harriet Tubman—the famous Underground Railroad conductor, military strategist, and informant— wasn't sure that she was going to see the end of slavery, but she carried her people forward anyway, for the benefit of future generations.

Critical to hope-making is the knowledge that the people around you will help you move forward, even when you have doubts. A few years ago, I visited Concourse Village Elementary School in the South Bronx. Alexa Sorden is the school's founding principal.

Walking through the hallways of Concourse Village Elementary School reminded me so much of my first day at Marva Collins Preparatory School. I started talking not only with Principal Sorden and the Concourse Village teachers, but with some of her students. Sebastian, who was eight years old and a third grader, was teaching a lesson on human rights when I visited his classroom. I asked him what he preferred, when students taught or when teachers did. He responded, clearly and confidently, that he preferred when students taught. "We get to say what we think, because the teachers already know this. They've already passed college and this. So we need to learn more and we can tell them what we think. And if we need help with it, then they can come and we can do a mini lesson with them, and they can help us."

When I asked Principal Sorden—who wrote the curriculum herself when she founded Concourse—about the straw man argument in the education community that often pitted culturally responsive teaching against rigor, she laughed before saying, "When I think about culturally responsive teaching, I always think about high expectations and how students are learning. I think about: How are my students reflected in that curriculum? I think about the 'So what?' aspect that Gloria Ladson-Billings talks about. The 'So what, why am I learning this? What does this mean for me?' And I don't see how you could not have both. Rigor, interest, and relevance, they all go hand in hand."

The human rights unit Sebastian was teaching came after the third-grade class had learned about the Bill of Rights and constitutional amendments. When looking at the amendments, Principal Sorden told me the students had a lot of questions like, "What is a warrant?" and "Why would someone need a warrant to search your home?" The class talked about the right to privacy and the right to protect your home from unjust search and seizure. "For a child to know that translates in so many ways, to not just your home, but your self, your being. How do you protect yourself as a human being? Which is what our human rights module is about. And now they're unpacking the Universal Declaration of Human Rights and connecting that to history. What did it mean to be a woman? And how did it play a role in where we are today? What was the industrial revolution and what role did children play? And when you look at the Universal Declaration of Human Rights, one of the rights is the right to play. How does that connect to who you are today? Bridging all of those connections [is important]."

Principal Sorden and her team knew that for Black and brown children, this topic of human rights was not only relevant, but key to building their knowledge and agency from a young age. As she said to me, "How does this curriculum extend beyond the classroom walls? When you think about cultural relevance, that's what it's about." Principal Sorden and her teachers were also clear that empowering their students required them to all be reading and writing on or above grade level and ensuring their fluency with numeracy and mathematical concepts. Was Concourse Village Elementary School perfect? No, but Alexa Sorden and her staff's pursuit of GLEAM there was so inspiring that it refreshed me and the vision I had for what was possible.

Alexa Sorden's school is a part of an incredible community of educators who have decided that the status quo is just not enough. She, like you and so many other educators across the country, is choosing hope, making a plan to enact grade-level, engaging, affirming, and meaningful pedagogy, and recalibrating along the way, with *justice is found in the details of teaching and learning*® as the North Star.

Centering Curiosity and Mindsets

I hope, if nothing else, that you will walk away from this book centering curiosity and hope in your practice as an educator. I know some of you might read this as a cop-out. "We need people to *change!*" you'll say, and you are right. I *also* want every educator and education

leader—regardless of race or ethnicity—to change. I want the systems
we live under to change today, yesterday if I could manage it. But it
is not an either/or proposition; rather it's a both/and approach to
centering justice in the details of teaching and learning. My own
journey toward equity has only been possible through a combination
of adaptive and technical means. It is no coincidence that committing
to adaptive change in our teaching and learning is one of our five
charges. The adaptive shift—the mindsets and curiosity—was both the
preamble and the driving force behind my technical shifts to develop a
classroom and organizational practice that prioritized a GLEAM lens.

For many years, I didn't question why I was so moved by the
intellect of the Black students I encountered. These were children
who looked like me, who went to schools like the one I attended,
whose parents looked like mine, and whose cultures mirrored mine in
so many ways. And yet, the many environments I had moved through
in my life taught me that these Black students were somehow an
anomaly. I never questioned where my ideas came from. The truth
was that images of Black intellect and Black brilliance were either
hidden or obscured throughout my early academic career; I lived all
of my life in a society that made Black success a rarity. It wasn't until
I became curious, that I began to ask: *Why are the statistics about Black
educational success like this? Why are the systems set up in this way? Who
stands to gain from me thinking I am the exception and not the rule?*

Curiosity is the tool that helps us uncover the biases that undergird
our thinking and our assumptions. Every time you ask why, you are
actively working to clear the smog of racism and inequity we have all
ingested. More importantly, when you keep asking questions, patterns
emerge, and those patterns make the solutions to systemic inequity—
the technical change—more obvious. However, technical shifts do not
guarantee sustained change. We need both adaptive change *and*
technical change—the former focused on shifting our thinking and
the latter centered on shifting our practices—if we want to attend to
the urgent task at hand: delivering justice through education.

Prioritizing curiosity and hope in your teaching, work, and learning also allows you to find your community. Not everyone is committed to the adaptive changes—the mindset shifts—needed to upend inequity, but the ones who are will find you and you will find them. Even knowing we're together on a hero's journey, seeking justice, encountering naysayers along the path is always hard. Professional trauma and hostility—the kind I endured as a new teacher trying to implement something beautiful and later inflicted as a school leader legislating the end of a middle school "graduation"—is real. The weariness is real. But as my colleague Brandon White reminds me, the burden of that trauma isn't as heavy when you find like-minded people who help you stay focused on the vision. As Brandon says, when we are focused on the vision and not just the system, we can continue this work of justice in a way that is self-sustaining. And if you can't find your community where you are, you will always have a place within the UnboundEd ecosystem, where we all believe that *justice is found in the details of teaching and learning*.

My dream is that, through all of our work—both individual and collective—we are creating pathways toward the complete dismantling and eradication of racism for future generations. It is a huge, multigenerational undertaking, but it's the justice we all deserve. We are the coalition of the willing and when we unite no one can stop us.

CONCLUSION

It might surprise you to know that at the beginning of my educational career, I was on the path to illiteracy. I've shared that my grandmother, born in the segregated South, was unable to read until she was in her sixties. I had the great honor of being one of my grandmother's first literacy teachers, but it almost didn't happen.

You see, at the end of my first-grade year, my mom got my final report card, announcing I had been promoted to the second grade. But she always says now that she got sick to her stomach when she saw that report card, because she knew I didn't know how to read. I was going to be pushed forward into the second grade without the foundational skill of literacy. She was immediately terrified that her own daughter could quite possibly be headed down the same pathway to illiteracy that she watched her mother struggle down throughout her entire life. Without even knowing the research or the science of reading, my mother knew I was missing a cornerstone in my education. So, my mother decided to get bold in her speech and show up at the school the next day. What she heard from the teachers was what a nice and quiet child I was. I was a "good" kid, they told her. But my mother didn't want to hear it; she understood that my sister and I were already fighting an uphill battle by integrating into a school system and neighborhood that had, at most, three families of color. She had already watched as white flight had drained our last neighborhood of educational resources, and she would not let this move—and her sacrifice to leave a community she loved—be in vain.

She told them, "Nice and quiet is not going to teach her how to read!" You see, like Mitchell, I had teachers who didn't see me in my entirety as a child, who made assumptions around my capabilities, and, dare I say, explicitly believed that as a young compliant student I would make do with my dismal literacy level. As a young Black girl, my amiability and compliance were valued over my learning. When Mitchell was adding call and response to his experience of *The Three Billy Goats Gruff,* he was deepening his own learning. But he wasn't quiet or compliant in the ways that racial biases, both implicit and explicit, tell us Black and brown children should be in order to be deemed as "good" and because of this, his learning was interrupted with the threat of discipline. My own niceness and quietness fit neatly into the mold of how society thought and, in some cases, still believes Black children *should* behave and because of this, my teachers didn't feel the need to push further or to ensure I was actually learning what I was being taught. My grandmother's illiteracy was a direct outcome of systemic racism and targeted laws. And while there were not any laws preventing me from learning how to read in my childhood, that same systemic racism colored my teachers' beliefs about the abilities and intellect of a little Black girl. My compliance was valued over my true readiness for the next grade and over my ability to unlock the code of literacy. Although I didn't have the same experience as my grandmother—the bolted-down barriers to her path to literacy—I experienced other barriers hinged on the beliefs that those educators felt about me and children like me. Now, I would be heedless if, as a seasoned educator, I didn't also reflect on the fact that, in addition to implicit and explicit biases, so many of us educators were not adequately prepared to support students in acquiring foundational educational skills like math and literacy. This is not due to lack of concern, but is instead an outcome of the educator-preparation pathways we are placed in during our own matriculation. I want to ask you, what barriers do you have secured in your halls, in your classrooms, in your lessons, that are disrupting our students' path to educational success and liberation? What negative systems have been erected that ensure continued cycles of inadequate teacher preparation? Because the truth is, they exist, whether you acknowledge them or not. And no, you didn't put them all up. Many of them were there before you first entered your classroom. But you—you and the community of the willing you're building—are going to have to be the ones that remove them.

When I finally learned how to read, reading became an insatiable appetite for me. I was reading everything I could get my hands on. When I got in trouble, my mother would threaten to take my books away. Nothing else moved me in the way words and stories did; to this day that remains true. Books became so critical to my life that I worked at the library from fifth grade until I graduated from high school. In my ninth-grade year, I remember my sister coming back from her first year of college at an HBCU. I was a huge V.C. Andrews fan at the time, but she told me, "You know, you should really pick up Maya Angelou or try Toni Morrison." So I did. I cannot tell you what *I Know Why the Caged Bird Sings* did for me. That same year, a young high school English teacher told me I should read *The Bluest Eye*; it literally opened up my soul. Finally, for the first time in my reading life, there were words on a page that encouraged me to examine my whole self. They awakened a part of me that I didn't even know was asleep. So now, when I hear on the news about school boards, elected officials, and parents who are campaigning to ban the very books that literally gave me freedom, I shudder. When those parents approach the podium at school board meetings, I see their anger, frustration, and fear. They are afraid that their children will be left in an environment that diminishes them. And I am struck by the fact their voices outweigh the generations of Black, Indigenous, and brown parents—parents like my mother—who have done nothing but beg this country to see their children as whole, beautiful, and brilliant. The unfounded fears of those parents at the podiums trump the righteous cries for justice in educational spaces, the desire for Black and brown children to be seen for who they are and who they could be. This current educational rhetoric is a direct outgrowth of what I saw on that television on the morning of January 6, 2021, when another angry mob was literally pushing our democracy into an abyss. And yet, very few people in positions of power in education are pausing to question and challenge this thinking. We have decades of data that chart economic disparities by zip code, disproportionate discipline by race, and systematic disenfranchisement at every level for Black, Indigenous, and brown students and their families. But where is that data that shows white children are being shamed in schools? It doesn't exist. On the contrary, the data seems to tell us that exposure to honest conversations about race and encountering diverse texts benefits white children as well as children of color.[1] Every day, we—the educators who are working to center justice in teaching and learning—are defending and expanding the rights of Black, Indigenous, Latinx, other students of color, and students experiencing poverty to access the education they deserve. The work of justice requires constant vigilance; it requires us to heed Horace Mann's original call that education is a tool by which the creeds of this nation can actually be lived. Mann said, "Without undervaluing any other human agency, it may be safely affirmed that the Common School . . . may become the most effective and benignant of all forces of civilization."[2] The call we're carrying has been handed to us through history, by educators with fewer means, living under more repressive governments. So I ask you as you build out your daily lesson plans, as you schedule your parent teacher conferences, as you head into that staff meeting, and as you show up to your school board meetings that you make three commitments.

First, **do not look away.** If we are going to be able to develop a plan of action, we must bear witness to the realities our students and colleagues face. We must stay curious about what we're seeing and why the systems we live in are structured this way. We cannot look away. Second, **be bold in your speech.** I can't imagine how different my life would have been if my mother had not gone up to the school that day after getting my first-grade report card and decided to boldly call out the teachers whose low expectations were erecting barriers in my education. Be that bold—bolder even—in the rooms you have access to.

Finally, **be bold in your actions.** Enacting grade-level, engaging, affirming, and meaningful teaching in your classroom is a bold action in a system mired in the status quo. That status quo will tell us that building classrooms which tolerate the Mitchells (and even the Laceys) of the world is enough; be bolder. Cultivate classroom environments where Black and brown children know they are not simply tolerated, but they are needed, their voices and learning are essential, and their experiences and communities are important. Demanding that your students have both the rigor and relevance they deserve is one of the boldest actions you can make in your career. Do it, proudly and without fear. Thank you for joining me and UnboundEd on this journey to justice. I am so grateful to be in community with you as Justice Seekers who are pursuing equity in the details of teaching and learning.

TOOLKIT PAGE

Seeking more UnboundEd resources and tools to center justice in the details of teaching and learning? Start by looking into our UnboundEd Anti-Bias Toolkit:

https://www.unbounded.org/educator-resources/ toolkits/anti-bias-toolkit

NOTES

Introduction

1. Rothwell, J. (2020, December 8). *Assessing the Economic Gains of Eradicating Illiteracy Nationally and Regionally in the United States.* Gallup. https://www.barbarabush.org/wp-content/uploads/2020/09/ BBFoundation_GainsFromEradicatingIlliteracy_9_8.pdf.

Chapter 1: Educational Inequity: How We Got Here

1. Nowicki, J. (2018). "Discipline Disparities for Black Students, Boys, and Students with Disabilities," U.S. Government Accountability Office.
2. Civil Rights Data Collection (2014). "Data Snapshot: Early Childhood Education." U.S. Department of Education.
3. Bacher-Hicks, A., Billings, S., and Deming, D. (2019). "The School to Prison Pipeline: Long-Run Impacts of School Suspensions on Adult Crime." Working Paper Series, no. w26257. Cambridge, MA: National Bureau of Economic Research.
4. Mann, A. (n.d.). "Touching the Spirit: The Two-Part Framework," *Augusta Mann's Touching the Spirit*^{TM}. Retrieved September 22, 2021, from http://successfulteachers.com/touching-the-spirit/.
5. Cf. Ladson-Billings, G. (2009). *The Dreamkeepers: Successful Teachers of African American Children.* Hoboken, NJ: John Wiley & Sons.

6. Linné, C. von. (1806). *A General System of Nature, through the Three Grand Kingdoms of Animals, Vegetables, and Minerals, Systematically Divided into Their Several Classes, Orders, Genera, Species, and Varieties, with their Habitations, Manners, Economy, Structure, And Peculiarities.* 10th ed., trans. W. Turton. Lackington, Allen, and Co.

7. Kendi, Ibram X. (2016). *Stamped from the Beginning: The Definitive History of Racist Ideas in America.* Bold Type Books, 50.

8. Williams, H. A. (2005). *Self-Taught: African American Education in Slavery and Freedom.* University of North Carolina Press.

9. Ibid.

10. General Assembly, "An Act to Amend the Act Concerning Slaves, Free Negroes and Mulattoes (April 7, 1831)" (2020, December 07). *Encyclopedia Virginia.* https://encyclopediavirginia.org/entries/an-act-to-amend-the-act-concerning-slaves-free-negroes-and-mulattoes-april-7-1831.

11. Span, C. M. (2009). *From Cotton Field to Schoolhouse: African American Education in Mississippi, 1862–1875.* University of North Carolina Press.

12. Williams, *Self-Taught.*

13. Douglass, F. (1969). *My Bondage and My Freedom.* New York: Dover Publications.

14. Rhode, D., Cooke, K., and Himanshu, O. (2012, December 19). "The Decline of the 'Great Equalizer.'" *The Atlantic.* https://www.theatlantic.com/business/archive/2012/12/the-decline-of-the-great-equalizer/266455/.

15. Apple, M. (1985). *Education and Power.* Boston: Routledge & Kegan Paul.

Chapter 2: Witnessing and Signifying: How Lenses Shape Our Teaching

1. Williams, H. A. (2005). *Self-Taught: African American Education in Slavery and Freedom.* University of North Carolina Press.

2. Givens, J. R. (2021). *Fugitive Pedagogy: Carter G. Woodson and the Art of Black Teaching*. Harvard University Press.

3. Williams, *Self-Taught*.

4. Ibid.

5. Troost, W. (2006). "Forty Acres and a School Freedmen's Bureau and Black Literacy Rates." UCI Graduate Student Seminar. University of California at Irvine.

6. Williams, *Self-Taught*.

7. Ibid.

8. Ibid.

9. Ibid.

10. Ibid.

11. Ibid.

12. Ibid.

13. Ibid.

14. Ibid.

15. Watkins, W. H. (2001). *The White Architects of Black Education: Ideology and Power in America: 1865–1954*. Teachers College Press.

16. Ibid.

17. Watkins, *The White Architects of Black Education*.

18. White, B., host. (2019). "The Complexion of Teaching and Learning." The Complexion of Teaching and Learning. *UnboundEd Blog*. https://blog.unbounded.org/the-complexion-of-teaching-and-learning/.

19. Ibid.

20. Ibid.

21. Williams, *Self-Taught*.

22. Au, W., et al. (2016). *Reclaiming the Multicultural Roots of U.S. Curriculum: Communities of Color and Official Knowledge in Education*. Teachers College Press.

23. White, "The Complexion of Teaching and Learning."

24. Gould, S. (1980). *Mismeasure of Man*. New York: W.W. Norton & Company.

25. Fairclough, A. (2006). "The Costs of *Brown*: Black Teachers and School Integration." *The Journal of American History*, 91 (1): 1–12.

26. National Center for Education Statistics. (2021, May). "Characteristics of Public School Teachers." https://nces.ed.gov/programs/coe/indicator/clr#.

27. Hussar, B., Zhang, J., Hein, S., Wang, K., Roberts, A., Cui, J., Smith, M., Bullock Mann, F., Barmer, A., and Dilig, R. (2020). "The Condition of Education 2020" (NCES 2020-144). U.S. Department of Education. Washington, DC: National Center for Education Statistics. Retrieved July 22, 2022. https://nces.ed.gov/pubsearch/pubsinfo.asp?pubid=2020144.

28. Lorde, A. (1984). The Master's Tools Will Never Dismantle the Master's House (Comments at the "The personal and the political panel," Second Sex Conference, New York, September 29, 1979). In *Sister Outsider* (pp. 110–113). Sister Visions Press. (Original work published 1979.)

29. Murrell, P. C., Jr. (2002). *African-Centered Pedagogy: Developing Schools of Achievement for American Children*. State University of New York Press.

Chapter 3: Learning at the Intersections: Race and Standards

1. Roberts, S. (2015, June 28). "Marva Collins, Educator Who Aimed High for Poor, Black Students, Dies at 78." *New York Times*. https://www.nytimes.com/2015/06/29/us/marva-collins-78-no-nonsense-educator-and-activist-dies.html.

2. Dave Bell Associates. *Success! The Marva Collins Approach*. Wilmette, IL: Television Licensing Center, 1984. Retrieved from https://www.youtube.com/watch?v=yXIDVjDlXpc.

3. The Reading League. (2022, January 10). *Science of Reading: Defining Guide.* https://www.thereadingleague.org/what-is-the-science-of-reading/.

4. Ibid.

5. Heifetz, R. A., and Linsky, M. (2002). "A Survival Guide for Leaders." *Harvard Business Review* 80(6): 65.

6. Collins, M., and Tamarkin, C. (1990). *Marva Collins' Way.* Los Angeles: Jeremy P. Tarcher.

7. Ball, D. L. (2018, April). "Just Dreams and Imperatives: The Power of Teaching in the Struggle for Public Education." In Presidential address at 2018 American Educational Research Association Annual Meeting. New York.

8. Ladson-Billings, G. (2006). "'Yes, But How Do We Do It?': Practicing Culturally Relevant Pedagogy." In Landsman, J., and Lewis, C. (Eds.). *White Teachers/Diverse Classroom: Creating Inclusive Schools, Building on Students' Diversity, and Providing True Educational Equity.* Sterling, VA: Stylus Publishing, 29–42.

9. Ladson-Billings, "'Yes, But How Do We Do It?,'" 29–42.

Chapter 4: Legacies and Lenses

1. Ladson-Billings, G. (2006). "'Yes, But How Do We Do It?': Practicing Culturally Relevant Pedagogy." In Landsman, J., and Lewis, C. (Eds). *White Teachers/Diverse Classroom: Creating Inclusive Schools, Building on Students' Diversity, and Providing True Educational Equity.* Sterling, VA: Stylus Publishing, 29–42.

2. Williams, M. A. (2001). *The 10 Lenses: Your Guide to Living and Working in a Multicultural World.* Capital Books.

3. Ibid.

4. Delpit, L. (1988). "The Silenced Dialogue: Power and Pedagogy in Educating Other People's Children." *Harvard Educational Review* 58 (3): 282. http://lmcreadinglist.pbworks.com/f/Delpit+(1988).pdf.

5. Benner, K., Medina, J., and Taylor, K. (2019, March 12). "Actresses, Business Leaders and Other Wealthy Parents Charged in U.S. College Entry Fraud." *New York Times*. https://www.nytimes.com/2019/03/12/us/college-admissions-cheating-scandal.html?action=click&module=inline&pgtype=Homepage.

6. Hannah-Jones, N. (2016, June 23). "What Abigail Fisher's Affirmative Action Case Was Really About." *ProPublica*. https://www.propublica.org/article/a-colorblind-constitution-what-abigail-fishers-affirmative-action-case-is-r.

7. West, J. (n.d.). "Book Review: The 10 Lenses: Your Guide to Living and Working in a Multicultural World." *English That Works*. Retrieved July 6, 2022. https://www.englishthatworksinc.com/review-10-lenses.php.

8. Ladson-Billings, "'Yes, But How Do We Do It?,'" 29–42.

9. Ladson-Billings, G. (2014). "Culturally Relevant Pedagogy 2.0: a.k.a. The Remix." *Harvard Educational Review* 84 (1): 74. https://www.cue.pitt.edu/sites/default/files/images/Source%205%20-%20ladson-billings%20culturally%20relevant%20pedagogy%20-%20the%20remix.pdf.

10. Morrison, T. (1998, January 19). From an interview on *Charlie Rose*. Public Broadcasting Service. Retrieved July 28, 2022. https://charlierose.com/videos/17664.

Chapter 5: Overview of GLEAM

1. Delpit, L. (1988). "The Silenced Dialogue: Power and Pedagogy in Educating Other People's Children." *Harvard Educational Review* 58 (3): 296. http://lmcreadinglist.pbworks.com/f/Delpit+(1988).pdf.

2. Ibid., 285.

3. Ladson-Billings, G. (2006). "'Yes, But How Do We Do It?': Practicing Culturally Relevant Pedagogy." In Landsman, J., and Lewis, C. (Eds). *White Teachers/Diverse Classroom: Creating Inclusive Schools, Building on*

Students' Diversity, and Providing True Educational Equity. Sterling, VA: Stylus Publishing.

4. Ferlazzo, L. (2015, July 8). "'Culturally Responsive Teaching': An Interview with Zaretta Hammond." *Education Week.* https://www.edweek.org/teaching-learning/opinion-culturally-responsive-teaching-an-interview-with-zaretta-hammond/2015/07.

5. Ladson-Billings, "'Yes, But How Do We Do It?'"

6. Tatum, B. (2017). *Why Are All the Black Kids Sitting Together in the Cafeteria?: And Other Conversations About Race.* Rev. ed. Basic Books.

7. TNTP. (2020). "Learning Acceleration Guide: Accelerating Learning in the 2020–2021 School Year." https://tntp.org/assets/covid-19-toolkit-resources/TNTP-Learning-Acceleration-Guide-Updated-Nov-2020.pdf.

8. Achieve The Core. (2016, September 27). "Progressions Documents for the Common Core State Standards for Mathematics." https://achievethecore.org/page/254/progressions-documents-for-the-common-core-state-standards-for-mathematics.

9. Wiggins, A. (2020, November 20). "Supports vs. Modifications: What's the Difference?" *UnboundEd Blog.* https://www.unbounded.org/blog/supports-vs-modifications-whats-the-difference.

10. Willis, J. (2014, May 1). "Neuroscience Reveals That Boredom Hurts." *Phi Delta Kappan.* https://kappanonline.org/neuroscience-reveals-that-boredom-hurts-willis/.

11. TNTP. (2018). "The Opportunity Myth: What Students Can Show Us About How School Is Letting Them Down—and How to Fix It." https://tntp.org/assets/documents/TNTP_The-Opportunity-Myth_Web.pdf.

12. Ibid.

13. Raney, M. (1997). "Technos Interview: Jeff Howard." *Technos* 6 (2). https://www.efficacy.org/media/9601/jeffhowardtechnosinterview.pdf.

Chapter 6: GLEAM in Practice

1. Ladson-Billings, G. (2006). "'Yes, But How Do We Do It?': Practicing Culturally Relevant Pedagogy." In Landsman, J., and Lewis, C. (Eds). *White Teachers/Diverse Classroom: Creating Inclusive Schools, Building on Students' Diversity, and Providing True Educational Equity.* Sterling, VA: Stylus Publishing.

2. Apple, M.W. (2000). *Official Knowledge: Democratic Education in a Conservative Age.* New York: Routledge.

3. Dewey, J. (1997). *Experience and Education.* New York: Simon & Schuster.

4. Ladson-Billings, "'Yes, But How Do We Do It?'"

5. National Museum of the American Indian. (n.d.). "Native American Cultures and Clothing: Native American Is Not a Costume." *Smithsonian.* Retrieved July 5, 2022, from https://americanindian.si.edu/nk360/informational/cultures-and-clothing.

6. Lesson 7.2.2: Introducing Proportional Relationships with Tables [Sample Lesson Plan]. (n.d.). Open-Up Resources. Retrieved July 6, 2022, from https://access.openupresources.org/curricula/our6-8math/en/grade-7/unit-2/lesson-2/teacher.html#activity-2.

7. Ghosh, V. E., and Gilboa, A. (2014). "What Is a Memory Schema? A Historical Perspective on Current Neuroscience Literature." *Neuropsychologia,* 53: 104–114. Retrieved July 29, 2022 from https://www.sciencedirect.com/science/article/abs/pii/S0028393213003990.

8. WIDA (2020). "English Standards Development Framework, 2020 Edition, Kindergarten–Grade 12." Board of Regents of the University of Wisconsin System. https://wida.wisc.edu/sites/default/files/resource/WIDA-ELD-Standards-Framework-2020.pdf.

9. EL Education. (n.d.). "Getting Started with the EL Education K-8 Language Arts Curriculum." Retrieved July 28, 2022, from https://eleducation.org/resources/collections/getting-started-with-the-el-education-k-8-language-arts-curriculum#.

10. Peters, M. (2014). *Patient Zero: Solving the Mysteries of Deadly Epidemics*. Illustrated ed. Annick Press.

11. Grade 7: Language Arts: Module 2: Epidemics, Teacher Guide. 2nd ed, updated. (n.d.). EL Education Language Arts Curriculum. Retrieved July 28, 2022, from https://curriculum.eleducation.org/curriculum/ ela/2019/grade-7.

12. At the time of writing this book, some curriculum providers are on the precipice of taking culturally relevant teaching into deeper consideration in their material and text design.

13. National Research Council. (2012). *A Framework for K–12 Science Education: Practices, Crosscutting Concepts, and Core Ideas*. Washington, DC: The National Academies Press. Retrieved July 28, 2022, from https://doi.org/10.17226/13165.

Chapter 7: Our Equity Charge

1. Gonzales, D., López, F., and Wiener, R. (2021). *United We Learn: Honoring America's Racial and Ethnic Diversity in Education*. The Aspen Institute. https://www.aspeninstitute.org/wp-content/uploads/2021/10/ Aspen-Institute_UnitedWeLearn.pdf.

2. Ibid.

3. Ibid.

4. Civil Rights Data Collection (2014). "Data Snapshot: Early Childhood Education." U.S. Department of Education.

5. Gilliam, W., Maupin, A., Reyes, C., Accavitti, M., and Shic, F. (2016). "Do Early Educators' Implicit Biases Regarding Sex and Race Relate to Behavior Expectations and Recommendations of Preschool Expulsions and Suspensions?" Yale University Child Study Center. https://medicine .yale.edu/childstudy/policy-and-social-innovation/zigler/publications/ preschool%20implicit%20bias%20policy%20brief_final_9_26_276766 _54643_v1.pdf.

6. Karter, E. (2021, September 28). "Study Finds Discipline Disparities in Preschool Driven by Racial Bias." *Northwestern Now*. https://news.northwestern.edu/stories/2021/september/ study-finds-discipline-disparities-in-preschool-driven-by-racial-bias/.

7. Patrick, K., Socol, A., and Morgan, I. (2020). "Inequities in Advanced Coursework: What's Driving Them and What Leaders Can Do." The Education Trust. https://edtrust.org/wp-content/uploads/2014/09/ Inequities-in-Advanced-Coursework-Whats-Driving-Them-and-What-Leaders-Can-Do-January-2019.pdf.

8. Ibid.

9. Losen, D., and Martinez, P. (2020). "Lost Opportunities: How Disparate School Discipline Continues to Drive Differences in the Opportunity to Learn." The Civil Rights Project. https:// www.civilrightsproject.ucla.edu/research/k-12-education/ school-discipline/lost-opportunities-how-disparate-school-discipline-continues-to-drive-differences-in-the-opportunity-to-learn/Lost-Opportunities-REPORT-v17.pdf.

10. Brown, B. (2021). *Atlas of the Heart: Mapping Meaningful Connection and the Language of Human Experience*. Random House.

Conclusion

1. Gonzales, D., López, F., and Wiener, R. (2021). *United We Learn: Honoring America's Racial and Ethnic Diversity in Education*. The Aspen Institute. https://www.aspeninstitute.org/wp-content/ uploads/2021/10/Aspen-Institute_UnitedWeLearn.pdf.

2. Horace Mann, as quoted in Claudia Levin (1992). *Only a Teacher* (Series), PBS. https://www.pbs.org/onlyateacher/credits.html.

ABOUT THE AUTHOR

 **Lacey Robinson** is the President and Chief Executive Officer of UnboundEd and chair of the board for CORE Learning. She focused on literacy, equity, and adaptive school leadership for more than two decades as an early childhood and elementary teacher, turnaround middle school principal, and staff development specialist. As a servant leader, Lacey's life work aims to help educators, leaders, and practitioners ensure systemic, sustained change that is aligned to educational equity efforts at every level of systems and organizations.

At UnboundEd, we envision a world in which educators actively work together to dismantle systemic racism by providing grade-level, engaging, affirming, and meaningful instruction. UnboundEd balances adaptive changes in mindsets and beliefs with technical changes in knowledge and skill. We seek to build educators' and leaders' asset-based and anti-racist beliefs and behaviors that impact student achievement, instructional practice, and systemic change for students of color. When educators at every level of the system work together to build knowledge and skills around college- and career-readiness standards, anchored in aligned and equitable instructional practices, systemic change can occur to close the opportunity gap for students of color. To learn more, visit www.UnboundEd.org.

ACKNOWLEDGMENTS

As I sat down and began writing this book I could feel the room filling with my ancestors, known and unknown. I could hear the voices of my ancestral enslaved African and Indigenous family members, sheroes, and heroes, some of whom were my maternal grandparents and father, as well as close family and friends. I could feel the energy of all the pushing, prodding, coaching, difficult discussions, and messages of hope that I have received along my life and career paths from mentors, teachers, leaders, and griots of education. Also present were the lessons I learned from the children whom I have had the honor of guiding along their education pathways and their parents and guardians, who entrusted me with the most precious gift that they have been given. Most importantly, I could feel my mother's words: "No matter what, do *not* give up" as I sat many days looking at a blank page and in the moments I felt bare and open, as I wrote about my mistakes and misunderstandings about myself and the children that I served. I want to thank my sister "Bri," Besties, and many, many others who have cheered out loud and in silence, listened to my cries against injustice, and forced me to celebrate the wins.

I also want to thank and acknowledge the current village of superheroes I have the pleasure to work with: the UnboundEd/Core staff and facilitators are truly an amalgamation of teachers, leaders, researchers, mathematicians, reading and ELA experts, science and history pedagogues, purveyors of language acquisition standards and equitable methodology, social activists, andragogy designers, and living pedagogy primers. In particular I want to thank Shakiela Richardson, Brandon White, Steve Sebelski, Alice Wiggins, Deborah Peart, Jen Arberg, and the teachers and leaders who graciously shared their anecdotes of GLEAM™ instruction; Ms. Hannah Turner, Ms. Carvajal, Mr. Neto, Ms. Bonig, Mr. Bowman, and Ms. Parrish; and Ms. Alexa Sorden, who opened the doors of her school, Lydia Ramos-Mendoza and Nicole Young, for making the story of our UnboundEd vision come to life amidst these pages. Lastly, I want to thank you, the reader, whom I will assume—through your path as a professional, student, parent, or collective community member in our Edusphere—has joined with UnboundEd as we seek justice in the details of teaching and learning.

INDEX

Page numbers followed by *f* refer to figures.